IMAGES
of America

VIRGINIA
STATE PARKS

Visitors Enjoy Seashore State Park. Will Carson, first chair of the Virginia Conservation and Development Commission, stated: "I would rather build a park where the plain people of Virginia can spend a pleasant outing and find pleasure and recreation close to nature, than to build a great church or endow a cathedral." This philosophy guided the early development of the Virginia State Parks (VSP) system. (Photograph courtesy VSP Collection.)

On the Cover: Park visitors relax on the shores of the Potomac River at Westmoreland State Park. Virginia's state parks offer access to important water resources in Virginia, including the four largest lakes, major rivers, and the Chesapeake Bay. Parks feature some of the commonwealth's most spectacular scenery with geographic landforms such as the iconic "Horsehead Cliffs" pictured here. (Photograph courtesy VSP Collection.)

IMAGES
of America

VIRGINIA STATE PARKS

Sharon B. Ewing
Foreword by Joe Elton

ARCADIA
PUBLISHING

Published by Arcadia Publishing
Charleston, South Carolina

Library of Congress Control Number: 2010934350

For all general information, please contact Arcadia Publishing:
Telephone 843-853-2070
Fax 843-853-0044
E-mail sales@arcadiapublishing.com
For customer service and orders:
Toll-Free 1-888-313-2665

Visit us on the Internet at www.arcadiapublishing.com

HUNGRY MOTHER OPENING DAY, 1936. The crowd was estimated at over 5,000 for the ceremony. A motorcade of almost 100 automobiles with Gov. George C. Peery and other dignitaries traveled from Marion's train depot to the park. Park Boulevard was not completed, so they drove a narrow, graveled road to the ceremony. Twenty state police were needed to handle traffic and parking at the event. (Photograph courtesy Hungry Mother State Park.)

CONTENTS

FOREWORD

Virginia's state parks were conceived in the Roaring Twenties, born during the Great Depression, expanded by baby boomers, and are ready to take on outdoor recreationists in the 21st century. Virginia preserves many of its most outstanding natural, cultural, and recreational treasures for the pure enjoyment of its citizens. Peace, relaxation, inspiration, and calm are sought and found in our parks. Nature's finest and history's best, along with the most outstanding outdoor recreation east of the Mississippi—hiking, biking, horseback riding, swimming, paddling, fishing, and so much more—await you in our award-winning state parks.

I am proud to work with hundreds of talented professionals who dedicate their lives to excellence in customer service and safety. They maintain our award-winning state parks—our cabins, campsites, beaches, trails, and historic structures—and bring great educational and entertaining programs to young and old alike. Generations of Virginians have celebrated special family events and holidays in their state parks. Continue the tradition and join the more than eight million visitors who make Virginia's state parks their outdoor recreation and vacation destination.

Years ago, I heard a park ranger say that life is nothing if not an adventure, and it is not so much the destination that we reach that is important but the journey along the way. Experience this walk through time, and be inspired by the dreamers who conceived and built these remarkable places. Take to heart the stewardship responsibility that we all have to protect our state parks for future generations. In Images of America: *Virginia State Parks*, you will come to understand why Virginians love their state parks and why we expect to find in them a special therapeutic tonic for the mind, body, and spirit.

Enjoy the journey.

—Joe Elton
Virginia State Parks Director

ACKNOWLEDGMENTS

This book builds upon earlier research and writing completed by others, particularly John Heerwald, retired director of Interpretive and Historic Programs. A number of fellow employees contributed support in several ways: Paula Hill, Warren Wahl, Nancy Heltman, Keith Morgan, Beth Roach, Ann Henderson, and Amy Atwood. A big "thanks" to Brenda Smith, who assisted tremendously. Park staff members that wrote and submitted park histories also deserve credit, as well as those who went to extra efforts to get information to me; these folks are too numerous to mention by name. Park families deserve a special thank you, especially my own; they provide support in many park endeavors. I also appreciate the assistance of Elizabeth Bray at Arcadia Publishing.

I am indebted to Joe Elton, state parks director, for writing the forward to the book and his support throughout the entire project. Also, much gratitude to members of the Virginia Association for Parks (VAFP), led by Johnny and Jo Finch, for their support of parks across Virginia. Proceeds from this book's purchase go to support the efforts of VAFP.

This book is an overview of 75 years of Virginia State Parks on both a public and institutional level. These historical images of parks across the system were taken from various sources, which are abbreviated as noted. These include the Department of Conservation and Recreation (DCR), various state parks (SP), the Virginia State Park Collection (VSP), the Library of Virginia (LVA), the Library of Congress, and various other collections.

INTRODUCTION

Virginia's effort to establish a park system gained momentum in 1926, when the Byrd administration created the Conservation and Development Commission. Led by William Carson, the commission sought to use Virginia's history to bring tourists and industry to the commonwealth and to establish it as a recreation hub. The commission's early efforts concentrated on support for Shenandoah and Colonial National Parks. Once these parks were underway, the commission focused on state park development. In December 1929, the Virginia Academy of Science, the Garden Club of Virginia, and the Izaak Walton League held a meeting in Richmond and passed a resolution in support of creating state parks. What Carson called a "skeleton organization," the Landscape Division headed by Robin "R. E." Burson was established to find suitable locations for park development.

In May 1930, officials toured a potential park tract near Cape Henry. In 1931, the Seashore State Park Association, a citizens' group, traveled with Burson to the National Conference on State Parks, which gave them a broader vision of the real value of state parks. Virginia hosted the conference in 1932, with the meetings held at Cape Henry's dunes. That same year, Burson was appointed as associate supervisor of the Virginia Division of State Parks. Under his guidance, the division gave hundreds of lectures and surveyed areas considered for state park development. By the spring of 1933, Burson had prepared the groundwork for creation of the Virginia State Park System.

What Carson called "the chance of a lifetime" presented itself when Pres. Franklin D. Roosevelt established the Civilian Conservation Corps in 1933. Carson was entertaining Roosevelt at Camp Rapidan near Shenandoah National Park. During that meeting, Carson proposed using the Civilian Conservation Corps to develop a system of state parks. The president replied, "I will give you the men and the money for your state parks, if you will demonstrate in Virginia what such a system of parks would mean to the state." Carson advised the national government that Virginia would take the camps as quickly as it could give them to the state.

Virginia had to provide land for the park sites. Just 15 days after the president's declaration, the Douthat Land Company donated a 1,920-acre tract along the Nelson River gorge in Bath and Allegheny Counties for Douthat State Park. Next, the Cape Henry Syndicate donated 1,100 acres for $1, including 1,000 feet of waterfront in Virginia Beach, for Seashore State Park. Marion businessmen John and Charles Lincoln, along with numerous other citizens of Smyth County, donated 2,500 acres of land for Hungry Mother State Park. Virginia's next state park materialized 10 days later. Junius Fishburn, publisher of the *Roanoke Times*, donated 5,000 acres in Patrick County that featured the unique geological formation known as the "Fairy Stone." On September 11, 1933, the Virginia General Assembly voted to allow the commission to acquire 1,226 acres along the Potomac for Westmoreland State Park at a maximum cost of $15,000.

The final acquisition of Staunton River State Park in Southside was more complicated. Carson insisted on the development of a swimming pool at the park, which held up funding. The approximate 1,200 acres, along the Staunton and Dan Rivers, were purchased by the commission. Halifax, Mecklenburg, and Charlotte Counties donated additional resources toward park acquisition.

On Saturday, June 13, 1936, Gov. George C. Peery presided over the opening ceremony for Virginia State Parks at Hungry Mother State Park in Marion. Thousands attended the celebration, which included band concerts, a water pageant, and a bathing beauty contest. Peery remarked on the opening of the system, "State parks are for all the people, and not only will they afford recreation for our own people but will bring tourists from other states. . . . I believe these parks will contribute greatly to the national good as we go forward." On the following Monday, June 15, 1936, the first six state parks in the system opened to the public. In the midst of the Great Depression, the opening of the state parks provided needed good news and brought jobs and economic opportunities in Virginia.

While the park system was off to a good start, the next two decades would prove to be challenging. The first park acquired after the initial six was Sailor's Creek Battlefield State Park in Amelia County. In the administration, due to political conflicts, both Carson and Burson were gone by 1939, and Randolph Odell was appointed commissioner. Also, in 1939, the agency assumed management of Goodwin Lake, Prince Edward, Holliday Lake, and Bear Creek Lake Recreation Areas.

With the outbreak of World War II, the Civilian Conservation Corps program ended on June 30, 1942. Due to gas shortages and restrictions on nonessential driving, none of the state parks opened in 1943. The developed parks reopened in 1944 and 1945, but visitation was low. By the war's end, operations resumed and visitation to Virginia's state parks was once again a priority for citizens. The commonwealth took possession of Swift Creek Recreation Demonstration Area, near Richmond, in 1946. Soon afterwards, it was renamed Pocahontas State Park. That same year, in far-western Virginia, the state acquired the Southwest Virginia Museum Historical State Park.

In 1948, property was acquired in Pulaski County for the development of Claytor Lake State Park. The Radford Chamber of Commerce developed and operated the property with minimal facilities. In 1949, a revenue bond provided monies for cabin construction in various parks. In 1951, after cabin construction at Claytor, the state took over operations. In 1954, Breaks Interstate Park was established as an "interstate park" on the Virginia and Kentucky border. Also, the initial property of Staunton River Battlefield State Park was acquired in 1955.

During this time, the system was evolving in a different way due to racial integration. In 1948, Maceo Martin, an African American, sought admission to Staunton River State Park and was refused. Martin filed suit, and according to the December 1948 board minutes, the commission decided to "expand the facilities of the Negro recreational area in Prince Edward County." In 1950, in keeping with the separate-but-equal doctrine, Virginia opened Prince Edward State Park for Negroes. The other state parks continued to serve whites only.

Another suit was filed in 1951 when African Americans were denied access to Seashore State Park. After the 1954 *Brown v. Board of Education* case, the state leased Seashore to a private operator and continued segregation. The state was unable to argue that the park was a private operation, and the plaintiffs were granted a court injunction. The state closed the park in 1955. In the following years, citizen groups pressured state officials to reopen Seashore. This resulted in an incremental reopening of park facilities from 1959 to 1963. Congress passed the Civil Rights Act in 1964 and effectively ended the policy of segregation in Virginia's state park system. In February 1965, funds were appropriated to refurbish Seashore's cabins, and the entire park was opened on an integrated basis.

From 1956 until 1963, no parks were added to the system. During this time, however, two other initiatives were undertaken. The first created the Natural Areas System in 1960 to preserve examples of Virginia's major landforms. Today the Natural Areas Preserve System is part of an ongoing effort to conserve Virginia's biodiversity. The second initiative began in 1962 under the new commissioner, Ben H. Bolen, who had been appointed in 1961. The system launched its interpretive program to foster understanding of the parks' diverse natural and cultural resources. Today programs are an essential part of the park visitor's experience.

In the late 1960s, the system began acquiring parks again to keep pace with population expansion. The Shot Tower (1964) and Grayson Highlands (1965) were both acquired. The 1965 Virginia Outdoors Plan, called "Virginia's Common Wealth," advocated for a long-range growth program.

In the following years, a number of parks were acquired: Smith Mountain Lake (1967), Natural Tunnel (1967), Mason Neck (1967), Chippokes Plantation (1967), False Cape (1968), Occoneechee (1968), York River (1969), Lake Anna (1972), Caledon (1974), Sky Meadows (1975), and Leesylvania (1975). Funding for staffing and facility construction lagged behind that for acquisition, and many of the new parks did not open for over a decade.

Ronald Sutton became state parks commissioner in 1982. The 1980s were a period of infrastructure and facility development. By 1989, all the parks acquired in the 1960s and 1970s had been opened to the public. Only one new park property was added during this time: in 1987, Norfolk Southern Corporation donated 57 miles of abandoned railroad right-of-way for New River State Park. Part of the national "Rails-To-Trails" movement, this acquisition gave Virginia its first linear state park.

In 1991, Dennis Baker became the VSP director (formerly the "commissioner" position). The VSP's "Virginia State Parks: Your Backyard Classroom" program for the Chesapeake Bay won the Environmental Protection Agency's 1991 Award for Environmental Education. Since then, the system has developed versions for the Piedmont and Mountain region parks. In 1992, Kiptopeke was acquired with Virginia Public Building Authority money. Voters also approved a $95 million bond for parks. Bond funds purchased the land and paid for the first phase of development for four new state parks: Belle Isle (1993), James River (1993), Wilderness Road (1993), and Shenandoah River (1994). Additionally, it funded the construction or renovation of campsites and cabins, as well the addition of numerous picnic shelters, boat ramps, visitor centers, amphitheaters, and other facilities. The 1955 Fort Hill property was expanded and became Staunton River Battlefield State Park.

In 1994, Joe Elton became Virginia's director of state parks. In the late 1990s, the agency undertook efforts to re-benchmark its operational funding. In 2002, voters overwhelmingly approved a $119 million bond. This funding resulted in the acquisition of additional park sites: Powhatan (2003), Seven Bends (2004), Widewater (2006), Middle Peninsula (2006), High Bridge Trail (2006), and Mayo River (2009). Additionally, it funded the construction of new cabins and family lodges, camping cabins, visitor centers, campgrounds, and equestrian campgrounds. In 2009, Virginia also acquired "Biscuit Run," 1,200 acres in Albemarle County, for future development.

Virginia State Parks continue to provide leadership in the parks and conservation field. In 2001, Virginia received the National Gold Medal for excellence in park management. The following year, the division initiated the VSP Youth Corps Program in 2002, which builds teenagers' leadership skills through conservation projects. New park construction uses "green" designs; a park visitor center was the first state-owned building to receive the Leadership in Energy and Environmental Design certification. In 2007, Virginia hosted the National Association of State Park Directors (NASPD) annual conference with a joint meeting of the National Park Service that resulted in the drafting of the Children and Nature Plan for Action, which challenged state and national parks to collaborate on ways to connect children with nature. In 2009, NASPD president Joe Elton led the national effort to promote America's State Parks and created an ASP Foundation.

In Images of America: Virginia State Parks, chapters are arranged chronologically by park development. The first chapter depicts the CCC era, while chapter two features the first six parks. The third chapter covers Sailor's Creek Battlefield, Bear Creek Lake, Holliday Lake, Twin Lakes, Southwest Virginia Museum, and Pocahontas State Parks. Chapter four features Claytor Lake, Staunton River Battlefield, Grayson Highlands, Smith Mountain Lake, Natural Tunnel, Mason Neck, Chippokes Plantation, False Cape, Occoneechee, and York River State Parks. Chapter five depicts Lake Anna, Caledon, Sky Meadows, Leesylvania, and New River Trail State Parks. Chapter six includes the parks of Kiptopeke, Belle Isle, James River, Wilderness Road, Shenandoah River, and High Bridge Trail. Finally, in chapter seven, readers meet a few "park people."

One

THE CIVILIAN CONSERVATION CORPS

RELOCATING RHODODENDRON AT HUNGRY MOTHER. During the Great Depression, Pres. Franklin D. Roosevelt created the Civilian Conservation Corps (CCC) to put unemployed men to work. Just 37 days after his inauguration, the first enrollees were inducted. These men would be sent to combat erosion and destruction of the nation's natural resources, leaving lasting legacies in parks and forests across the country. (Photograph courtesy Hungry Mother SP.)

STAUNTON RIVER CCC. Enrollees were unmarried and unemployed male U.S. citizens, 18–20 years of age. Each enrollee volunteered to serve six months to two years. They worked 40 hours per week, receiving $1 per day pay, food, clothing, housing, and medical care. Of his $30 in monthly pay, each enrollee was required to send $22–$25 home to a family dependent. (Photograph courtesy Staunton River SP.)

1373RD DOUTHAT BARRACKS. Each CCC camp was located at the park construction site. They were organized around a complement of up to 200 enrollees in a designated numbered company unit. Camps were structured with barracks for 50 enrollees each, officers/technical staff quarters, medical dispensary, mess hall, recreation hall, educational building, lavatory and showers, administrative offices, tool room/blacksmith shop, and motor pool garages. (Photograph courtesy Pocahontas SP.)

Hungry Mother Camp Officers. The enrollees formed work units of 25 men each, organized according to their barrack assignments. Each section had an enrollee leader and assistant leader who were accountable for the men both at work and in the barracks. Each camp had supervisors that were U.S. Army Reserve officers. (Photograph courtesy Hungry Mother SP.)

Douthat Camp Officers. The military officers were responsible for camp operation, logistics, education, and training. There were also 10–14 technical service civilians, including a camp superintendent and foreman employed by the Departments of Interior or Agriculture. Camp operations included several other supervisors, who provided hands-on knowledge and guidance for inexperienced enrollees. (Photograph courtesy Pocahontas SP.)

Hungry Mother Tent Camp. Once men were assigned to a company, they were transported to the park. The first company would erect the camp where the men would live. At Hungry Mother, there was delay in building of the barracks, and the tent camp was used through an unusually cold fall. Civilian carpenters were hired to assist with the building of permanent barracks. (Photograph courtesy Hungry Mother SP.)

Hungry Mother Barracks. The first company was also responsible for establishing a water system, digging wells if needed, for a fresh water supply. They were required to construct the maintenance buildings to fabricate materials for the erection of the park structures on site. In addition, they built the roadways within the park. (Photograph courtesy Hungry Mother SP.)

FAIRY STONE CONVOY. The first CCC enrollees arrived in Bassett in October 1933. They slept in tents prior to constructing their barracks. They cut pine trees for use in the construction of the park buildings. Another task was to lay the pipes for the water system, drawing water from a small mountain reservoir. Additionally, they constructed the dam and harvested stone from borrow pits. (Photograph courtesy VSP Collection.)

WESTMORELAND WATER SUPPLY. Constructed in 1934 by the CCC, the park's original water source was a dammed pond. The dam had a concrete spillway emptying into a creek. Other structures included a water filtration plant and storage tower. The water tower is still in use, but the water source is now a well. (Photograph courtesy VSP Collection.)

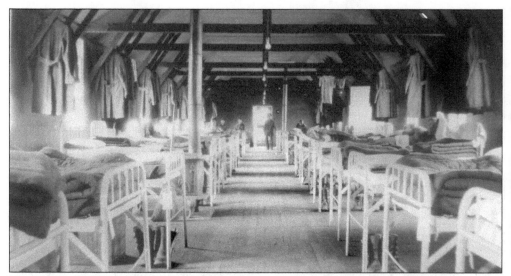

HUNGRY MOTHER BARRACK COTS. The men slept dorm-style in the barracks. The buildings were frame construction, covered with building paper on the outside, and sealed with Masonite inside. Some of the men who slept here had the last names of Pagano, Wieliewczky, Murdza, Hahan, Soia, Lebowicz, and Frascella. (Photograph courtesy Hungry Mother SP.)

DOUTHAT CAMP KITCHEN. "Three hots and a cot" was how enrollee Sam Solloway described the meals and housing provided. Solloway first worked quarrying stone for the Douthat dam spillway. Later he was transferred to the kitchen. Like most CCC members, Solloway joined the army during World War II. His camp training served him well; he spent a 31-year career in mess halls and canteens. (Photograph courtesy Pocahontas SP.)

STAUNTON RIVER MESS HALL. The camp workdays were scheduled much like the military, with reveille, three meals a day, and work. The day began approximately at 7:30 a.m. and ended at 4:00 p.m. After dinner, men could attend educational courses provided by teachers hired by the CCC, or participate in recreational activities. (Photograph courtesy Pocahontas SP.)

HUNGRY MOTHER OFFICERS HEADQUARTERS. Leading large groups of young, unmarried men kept company officers busy. Many of these men were far from home and working in areas that were culturally different from their backgrounds. Activities were organized for the men. These included company newsletters, talent shows, bands and chorale groups, art shows, and sporting events. (Photograph courtesy Hungry Mother SP.)

CCC BOYS ON EQUIPMENT. Construction, on the scale of the development of six parks, often required equipment. Unique in facility construction was the building of a pool and tennis courts at Staunton River State Park. None of the other five original parks offered these facilities. Transferred from Glacier National Park, Camp 1220 of Fort Niagara, New York, was assigned the task of constructing the pool. (Photograph courtesy VSP Collection.)

DOUTHAT LAKE CONSTRUCTION. Company 1373, Camp Carson, began construction the day after they set up camp on July 16, 1933. According to documentation, the design for Douthat's dam was also used at Hungry Mother and Fairy Stone. Lee H. Williamson, dam engineer, worked under the supervision of the Virginia Commission on Conservation and Development and the Department of the Interior's State Park Emergency Conservation Work. (Photograph courtesy LVA.)

DOUTHAT SPILLWAY. Dam construction, including supervision, supplies, materials, and equipment operation, cost $325,044.03. Included in this figure is $179,397.50 paid to CCC enrollees. The dam, which is approximately 600 feet long, was completed in July 1935. Additional masonry work to prevent erosion at the spillway opening was completed in October. The stone, which faces the spillway, was quarried within the park boundaries. (Photograph courtesy Pocahontas SP.)

FAIRY STONE LAKE CONSTRUCTION. Company 1260 arrived first with men from Yellowstone. Later they were joined by Companies 1267 and 1279. One camp came from Camp Dix (now Fort Dix), New Jersey, and was for young men from immigrant families of New York City and New Jersey boroughs. Some Virginia men worked at Fairy Stone, but an overwhelming number of the enrollees were from elsewhere. (Photograph courtesy VSP Collection.)

FAIRY STONE EQUIPMENT OPERATORS. CCC enrollee Ralph Hines recalled his time building Fairy Stone State Park. "I did drafting and blasting of rocks. . . . We also dug a lake, built cabins and roadways, and fought fires. On the weekends, a bus took us into Bassett. Some went to the movies for 15¢, . . . [and] we played basketball and baseball." (Photograph courtesy VSP Collection.)

HUNGRY MOTHER SPILLWAY. From 1933 to 1934, the dam and spillway were erected on Hungry Mother Creek. Companies 1252, 1249, and 1259 arrived to construct the park. Also arriving from work in Yellowstone, the men hailed from New York and New Jersey. Local men were also guaranteed work with the three companies. Companies 1252 and 1249 cleared the lake area and 1259 built the dam. (Photograph courtesy Hungry Mother SP.)

Tower Construction. Fairy Stone has a number of original CCC structures and retains its original design. The CCC constructed the following: the dam, roads, trails, water supply, nine cabins, beach, picnic shelters, and restrooms. They also placed tons of riprap and planted trees to repair erosion damage resulting from extensive area logging. (Photograph courtesy VSP Collection.)

Hungry Mother Lake Work. One of the purposes of the first six parks was to provide recreation. The lakes constructed by the Civilian Conservation Corps enabled the parks to provide water recreation such as swimming, fishing, and boating. These recreational activities required bathhouses and the construction of piers and boat ramps. (Photograph courtesy Hungry Mother SP.)

FAIRY STONE DAM. From 1934 to 1935, a 25-foot-high dam was erected over Goblintown Creek. The spillway was constructed of stone; the dam was earthen and is supported by stone. A concrete cross, resembling a Fairy Stone, was mounted on the west side of the dam. The resulting lake comprised 168 acres. (Photograph courtesy VSP Collection.)

FILLING FAIRY STONE LAKE. In 1936, Company 2337 took over from the original camps but was replaced shortly by Company 5436, with men from Georgia and Florida. Company 1389, whose members came from the Southwest and Valley regions of Virginia, replaced 5436. During their three years, they constructed buildings, horse trails, roads, and the campground. This final camp left the park in 1940. (Photograph courtesy VSP Collection.)

TRAIL CONSTRUCTION. Another integral part of the parks' development was the creation of a trail system. Hiking allowed visitors to view the natural beauty of the park. The trails were developed based upon available land and accessibility. (Photograph courtesy Hungry Mother SP.)

BALD CYPRESS TRAIL. Early references to the land developed as Seashore State Park referred to it as the "desert." It was considered unfit for tillage and cultivation and was therefore deemed uninhabitable. To build the park, the CCC had to clear undergrowth, cut roads and trails, and build bridges and boardwalks over the marshlands. (Photograph courtesy VSP Collection.)

BRIDGE CONSTRUCTION.
Craftsmanship was a hallmark
of Civilian Conservation
Corps structures. Logs felled
from the surrounding forest
were used to construct cabins,
lodges, picnic shelters, and
trail bridges. (Photograph
courtesy Hungry Mother SP.)

DITCH CONSTRUCTION. Many
of the first parks' roads and
associated structures feature
Civilian Conservation Corps
stonework, including culverts,
retaining walls, and stone-
lined ditches. An example
of CCC craftsmanship is the
original parking areas at Hungry
Mother. The stone curbing
takes the shape of various tools
used during the construction
of the park, including a hoe
and shovel. (Photograph
courtesy VSP Collection.)

STAUNTON RIVER CABIN. There were eight CCC cabins constructed from 1934 to 1936. The structures had fieldstone foundations, and a frame construction clad in board-and-batten siding. Each cabin had a stone fireplace and chimney with rustic wood mantles. Electricity was not initially provided in Staunton River State Park for cabin guests. It was added in 1941 and primarily used for lighting. (Photograph courtesy Staunton River SP.)

SEASHORE RESTAURANT. Of the three original camps sent to build Seashore State Park, one was African American. From the beginning of the CCC, African Americans participated in segregated camps. The Big "H" Complex was a half-timbered building constructed during the park's CCC era, 1933–1942, for use as a restaurant and administration building. (Photograph courtesy VSP Collection.)

DOUTHAT LODGE CONSTRUCTION. Company 1374, Camp Douthat, built the cabins and lodge. The lodge was to house overnight park visitors, since at the time, the cabins were available only to those who wished to stay a minimum of one week. Four of Douthat's original buildings were included in an NPS training manual for construction workers in national and state parks. (Photograph courtesy LVA.)

CLEARING LAND. The original parks' sites were distributed throughout the state to represent the four largest physiographic regions of Virginia. The topography of these properties varied, but at each of them, much backbreaking work had to be done. Without the labor force provided by the Civilian Conservation Corps, Virginia's first six parks would not have been ready to launch in 1936. (Photograph courtesy VSP Collection.)

Two

VIRGINIA'S FIRST
SIX PARKS

DOUTHAT SIGN. The present-day Douthat State Park was part of a land patent granted to Robert Douthat in 1795. The land changed owners numerous times over the next 135 years. In 1933, the Douthat Land Company donated 1,920 acres for the creation of a park. Later that year, 2,573 more acres were purchased with Virginia General Assembly parkland acquisition monies. (Photograph courtesy VSP Collection.)

DOUTHAT LODGE. The CCC cabins were completed in two stages: cabins 1–9 and cabins 19–21 were completed in 1935, and cabins 10–18 and 22–25 were completed in 1936. The lodge featured six bedrooms with three stone terraces and was completed in 1935. It displayed the same rustic character of the cabins but on a grander scale. (Photograph courtesy VSP Collection.)

GUESTS INSIDE LODGE. The lodge is a craftsman's masterpiece. The wood and stone interior is architecturally pleasing. The living room ceiling has a five-arch support of exposed beams. It also has handwrought hardware on the shutters, doors, and beams. (Photograph courtesy LVA.)

DOUTHAT BEACH. The park's swimming area is the location of the "borrow" pit for earthen material used during dam construction. A beach and bathhouse were constructed at the pit site. The bathhouse, which is now the beach house and conference center, was completed in 1938 and is the only two-story building in the park. (Photograph courtesy DCR.)

DOUTHAT TRAIL. In modern times, the park has 30 cabins, two lodges, a 50-acre lake, three campgrounds, a beach, conference center, boat launch, and a restaurant. There are 25 trails, which provide a total of 43 miles of hiking trails—all but 3 of these miles were originally built by the Civilian Conservation Corps. (Photograph courtesy DCR.)

SEASHORE (FIRST LANDING). In July 1931, the Seashore State Park Association was chartered in Norfolk. The group's goal was to encourage the acquisition of lands for the creation of a state park at the seashore. The site at Cape Henry had become a popular tourist attraction due to its association with the landing of the first settlers. (Photograph courtesy VSP Collection.)

SEASHORE TRAILHEAD. Cape Henry is a large sand spit formed by wave movement. As the sand was pushed northward, water was trapped between the mainland and the oceanfront. This created a maritime forest with swamps inland from the sand dunes. The plant life here is the northernmost point for plants that are indigenous to a Southern climate. (Photograph courtesy VSP Collection.)

BALD CYPRESS TRAIL. Cypress and fresh water springs provided fuel and water for travelers to early settlements along the Chesapeake Bay. This area was held by various landowners in the 1700s but was used as public property from 1770 until after the Civil War due to its importance for sailors and watermen. (Photograph courtesy VSP Collection.)

SEASHORE STATE PARK. From 1866 to 1899, the land saw various owners. In 1899, it was sold to the Cape Henry Syndicate, who timbered and quarried sand from the land. On August 8, 1933, the syndicate donated 1,100 acres for the creation of the park. In 1934, the state purchased the remaining portion of the parkland for $260,000. (Photograph courtesy VSP Collection.)

SEASHORE CABIN GUESTS. Among the first six state parks in Virginia, Seashore's cabins deviated from the popular log cabin form seen at the other parks. These buildings reflected a simpler style, indicative of a warmer climate. (Photograph courtesy VSP Collection.)

FIRST LANDING BEACH. In early years, Seashore was the second-most popular park, behind Hungry Mother. Due to its proximity to large population areas, today the park receives the highest attendance. In the 1990s, interest arose in changing the park's name to one that emphasized its historic significance. The name of Seashore State Park formally changed to First Landing State Park in 1995. (Photograph courtesy VSP Collection.)

HUNGRY MOTHER SIGN. John and Charles Lincoln, landowners and entrepreneurs, saw the potential park as an economic boom to Smyth County. Along with other landowners and community leaders such as Frank Copenhaver and Robert Anderson, the Lincolns took a direct interest in the prosperity of the park. Each worked closely with Will Carson, R. E. Burson, and Richmond officials to guide the park's progress during construction. (Photograph courtesy Hungry Mother SP.)

BEACH ARIEL. The park's beach provided unusual recreation in mountainous Southwest Virginia. The sand was provided by John Lincoln and transported from Virginia Beach. Another unique feature was the park's name. During development, several names were considered, including Forest Lake, Royal Oak, and Walker's Park. Officials were taken with a local legend and thus christened the new park as Hungry Mother State Park. (Photograph courtesy Hungry Mother SP.)

BEACH. One variation of the legend is this: in the 1700s, the Marley family was attacked by Native Americans. The father was killed; his wife, Molly, and their child were captured. They escaped, but on the journey home, Molly starved to death. A hunting party found them near a creek; the child was crying, "Hungry, mother, hungry." The creek became "Hungry Mother Creek," and a nearby peak, "Molly's Knob." (Photograph courtesy Hungry Mother SP.)

Interior Guest Lodge Restaurant
Hungry Mother State Park
Marion, Va.
Silverglo 2 A 100
BRISTOL, VA.

LODGE POSTCARD. When Hungry Mother opened in 1936, Dick Taylor was the park custodian. Operations were seasonal from Memorial Day to Labor Day, with the park hosting a grand reopening each year. The single campground was only for tent camping, and cabins offered only cold water and metered electricity. The park's original buildings included six cabins, the lodge, two shelters, and the restaurant. (Postcard courtesy Hungry Mother SP.)

EARLY RESTAURANT. Today Hungry Mother State Park features 20 cabins and four campgrounds. The lake offers swimming, boating, and fishing. A variety of trails provide recreation for hikers of all levels. A restaurant serves wonderful meals, and the Hemlock Haven Conference Center allows the park to host groups throughout the year. (Photograph courtesy VSP Collection.)

FAIRY STONE LAKE. The park is the former site of Union Furnace Ironworks, which was located under the current lake. The ironworks was founded in the early 1800s by the Hairston family and sold to Barksdale and Stovall, Confederacy agents, in 1863. It is likely that the iron used to clad the CSS *Virginia* (USS *Merrimac*) came from this ironworks. (Postcard courtesy LVA.)

PARK ENTRANCE. From 1905 until 1915, the ironworks operated the Virginia Ore and Lumber Company (VO&L). The name Fayerdale was given to the community that arose around the ironworks. In the early 1920s, a fire devastated the village, causing the railroad to cease its operation. Many people abandoned the community. (Photograph courtesy DCR.)

V-906 Water Sports on Lake at Fairy Stone State Park in Virginia

FAIRY STONE POSTCARD. In 1925, the entire tract was sold to Junius R. Fishburn, publisher of the *Roanoke Times* newspaper and one of the original investors of the Virginia Ore and Lumber Company, for $1 per acre. On October 20, 1933, he donated the entire tract to the Commission on Conservation and Development to develop one of Virginia's first six state parks. (Postcard courtesy VSP Collection.)

FAIRY STONES. The park is named for the staurolite crystals found there. The folded crystals appear in cross forms and are considered to bring good luck. A legend states that the "fairy stones" were created when fairies living in the region heard of the death of Christ; their tears fell on the stones and were crystallized into the cross-shaped forms. (Photograph courtesy LVA.)

FAIRY STONE BEACH. Visitors to Fairy Stone can enjoy nature and solitude while staying in one of the park's cabins or campsites. Fayerdale Conference Center is available for meetings and reunions. Multiuse trails are open for hiking, cycling, and horseback riding. Sunbathing and swimming are popular park pastimes. (Photograph courtesy DCR.)

WESTMORELAND CLIFFS. An estimated 15 to 25 million years ago, Westmoreland State Park was under a shallow sea teeming with marine life. Their remains can be found at the park. Fossils and the geologic formations created in the Miocene epoch are visible by viewing the area along the Horsehead Cliffs. (Photograph courtesy VSP Collection.)

WESTMORELAND CABIN. Originally part of the Cliffs Plantation patented by Nathaniel Pope around 1650, the land that is present-day Westmoreland State Park was owned by John Washington, grandfather of George Washington. The land was later purchased by Thomas Lee and became part of the estate of the birthplace of Robert E. Lee and two signers of the Declaration of Independence. (Photograph courtesy DCR.)

BOATING ON THE POTOMAC. On October 11, 1933, the creation of Westmoreland State Park became possible when Fred Nash sold 1,266.5 acres to the Commonwealth of Virginia for $15,000; the need to acquire land with river frontage was noted on early maps. Additional land was acquired in the 1940s and 1990s. The fishing pier and over a mile of shoreline offer fisherman and boaters multiple opportunities to enjoy the Potomac. (Photograph courtesy VSP Collection.)

INSIDE WESTMORELAND CABIN. The housekeeping cabins, camping cabins, and beautiful waterfront lodge are key features of the park. The park's 1,300 acres offer trails covering more than 7 miles with hiking opportunities from strolling to backcountry hiking. The park's scenic views of the Potomac may be enjoyed year round. (Photograph courtesy DCR.)

WESTMORELAND CAMPING. By the opening of Virginia's first state parks in 1936, camping trailers had been invented. Travelers were increasingly pulling these units, but tent camping remained popular. A typical campsite featured a fire ring, a picnic table, and room for pitching a tent. Today the park has three campgrounds offering standard and full services. (Photograph courtesy LVA.)

STAUNTON RIVER SIGN. In 1933, the commonwealth acquired 1,196.5 acres at the confluence of the Staunton and Dan Rivers for $10,000. Funding came from the state, and $2,500 was provided, in total, by the counties of Mecklenburg, Halifax, and Charlotte. The land was the former Fork Plantation site, comprised of farmland with timbered areas along the waterfront. (Photograph courtesy Staunton River SP.)

STAUNTON RIVER POOL. While the other first parks used either lakes or a river as the public swimming facility, the Dan and Staunton Rivers were thought to be too polluted for swimming, so William Carson requested the construction of a pool. The cost of the pool ($12,000) caused the National Park Service to initially refuse funding for it, but a pool was eventually approved in 1934. (Photograph courtesy DCR.)

STAUNTON RIVER WADING POOL. Carson had argued that, without a pool, the park would fail. The need for the park in this area of Virginia was to provide recreation, more for the local community than for outside tourists. The 150-foot-by-60-foot pool (complemented by a 40-foot diameter wading pool) was touted as the largest in the commonwealth. (Photograph courtesy DCR.)

STAUNTON RIVER "OPENING DAY" BEAUTY CONTEST. By the park's opening in 1936, the cabins, picnic areas, and swimming pool and bathhouse had been completed. In the first year, Staunton River State Park saw an attendance of 12,581 and had the third-highest park attendance of Virginia's first six state parks. (Photograph courtesy Staunton River SP.)

STAUNTON RIVER VISITOR CENTER. In 1952, with the completion of the John H. Kerr Dam and the formation of Buggs Island Lake, part of the park was flooded. This gave the park the benefit of being located on Virginia's largest lake with plentiful fishing. Park facilities included the visitor center, pool, tennis courts, picnic areas, playground, a boat-launching facility, campground, cabins, and nature trails. (Photograph courtesy Staunton River SP.)

Three

EARLY DEVELOPMENTS IN THE 1930S AND 1940S

SAILOR'S CREEK BATTLEFIELD SITE, 1936. April 6, 1865, marked the last major battle of the Civil War. Eight Confederate generals surrendered; the total of Southern casualties and prisoners reached 7,700 men. Upon seeing the survivors streaming along the road, Lee asked, "My God, has the army dissolved?" This battle was the Confederate army's death knell; Lee surrendered 72 hours later at Appomattox Courthouse. (Photograph courtesy NPS.)

HILLSMAN FARM, 1936. The battle included three distinct engagements, Hillsman's Farm, Marshall's Crossroads, and Lockett's Farm. The Hillsman Farm is preserved as Sailor's Creek Battlefield Historical State Park. Interest for the park's establishment began in 1934 when an association met for a battlefield picnic. This led to the Virginia General Assembly appropriating funds and acquiring the site in 1937. (Photograph courtesy LVA.)

HILLSMAN HOUSE, 1936. The 1700s Colonial home, known as the Hillsman House, was built by Moses Overton; an Overton descendent married John Hillsman. The house served as a field hospital. The main room's two beds and floor space were used to treat Union officers. The entry hall was used as an operating room, and both Union and Confederate wounded were treated on the lawn. (Photograph courtesy NPS.)

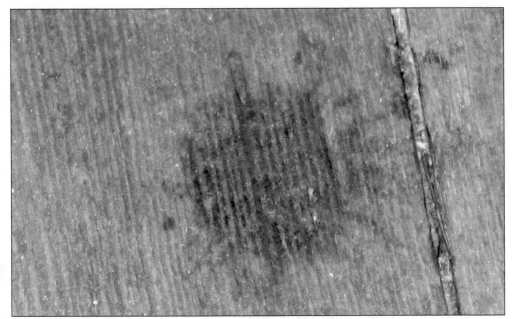

BLOODSTAINS. The floor of the Hillsman House bears bloodstains from its use as a hospital. Troops treated at the house include 358 Union and 161 Confederate soldiers. In 2008, a forensic unit investigated the bloodstains and documented their authenticity. Preservation methods now protect these historic reminders of soldiers' sacrifices. (Photograph courtesy Sailor's Creek Battlefield HSP.)

CEMETERY. Members of the Overton-Hillsman family are buried nearby. Whether the farm contains mass Confederate burials is unknown. The battle was a bloody scene. A 1st Vermont Cavalryman wrote, "The dead were virtually piled one upon another, and it was the last ditch of thousands." Only 45 of the dead were buried at Poplar Grove National Cemetery near Petersburg. (Photograph courtesy Sailor's Creek Battlefield HSP.)

BEAR CREEK LAKE, 1940S. The area known as Bear Creek Lake State Park was originally the Cumberland State Forest Recreation Area. The property was purchased by the U.S. Department of Agriculture through the Bankhead-Jones Farm Tenant Act, initiated by the Roosevelt Administration. The intent was to improve submarginal land that had been abused by poor farming and timbering practices. (Photograph courtesy Bear Creek Lake SP.)

BEAR CREEK LAKE DEVELOPMENT. About 100 men helped build Bear Creek Lake. Documentation about the various groups represented is sketchy, but it is believed to involve the Cumberland County Civilian Conservation Corps, Works Progress Administration forestry workers, local carpenters, and farmers. Construction work included clearing of lake timber, construction of the dam, and the building of two pavilions, a concession stand, and six fireplaces. (Photograph courtesy Bear Creek Lake SP.)

FORESTRY WORKERS. One worker recalled, "The winter of 1936 got so cold that the blacktop on Route 60 froze and buckled into a bone-shaking jumble. Donald Black was hired to timber-out the poor wood on land that became Bear Creek Lake Recreational Area. Tools provided by the Agriculture Department consisted of crosscut saws, bow saws, and axes. He provided his own boots and gloves." (Photograph courtesy Bear Creek Lake SP.)

BOATING, 1940s. In July 1939, the Virginia Conservation Commission signed an agreement with the U.S. Department of Agriculture to administer the recreation areas of Bear Creek, Holliday, Goodwin, and Prince Edward Lakes. The property was managed as a day-use area until 1962, when it was renamed Bear Creek Lake State Park, complete with camping facilities. In 2007, cabins were added to the overnight facilities. (Photograph courtesy VSP Collection.)

CONCESSION STAND. Louise Woolard remembers visiting the park: "The old concession building was perfect. . . . I loved the front that opened up to reveal all the goodies you could purchase. There were tee shirts and sweatshirts with big 'bears' on the front . . . and the popcorn always smelled so good. . . . The concessionaire would grill hot dogs and hamburgers, . . . and you could smell it all the way to the campground. Definitely 'smell' marketing!" (Photograph courtesy VSP Collection.)

HOLLIDAY LAKE. The area encompassing Holliday Lake State Park and the surrounding state forest was settled and farmed in the 1800s. During the Great Depression, the land was acquired by the U.S. Agriculture Department for development, similar to that of Bear Creek Lake. Between 1936 and 1939, approximately 100 local men were hired to develop roads, clear timber, and to build the dam and lake. (Photograph courtesy Virginia Tech Digital Library.)

WORKS PROGRESS ADMINISTRATION CAMP. The camp housed the workers who built Holliday Lake and reforested the area. It consisted of 15 eight-bunk cabins, built along ridges. A large activity building/dining hall sat atop a terraced area facing Holliday Lake. The intact WPA camp survives today because it became a 4-H camp in 1941. (Photograph courtesy Virginia Tech Digital Library.)

HOLLIDAY DAM. Construction of a dam was begun at Fish Pond Creek in 1937 and then relocated to Holliday Creek. After the 150-acre lake and the dam were completed in 1939, it became a day-use recreation area managed by the commonwealth known as the Surrender Grounds Forest. In 1972, with the addition of campgrounds, the recreation area became Holliday Lake State Park. (Photograph courtesy Holliday Lake SP.)

HOLLIDAY. The spelling of the park's name is a mystery. Most often, it appears with two "Ls." An 1834 hydrological map of the upper Appomattox River shows a "Holy Day Creek." Whatever the reason, "Holy Day Creek" changed over the years to "Holliday Creek," and the name was given to the lake when it was formed. (Photograph courtesy Holliday Lake SP.)

HOLLIDAY LAKE STATE PARK. The park's 255 acres are surrounded by the 19,000-acre Appomattox-Buckingham State Forest, the largest state forest in Virginia. Park visitors can enjoy a wide variety of outdoor activities, including swimming, boating, fishing, waterfowl watching, hiking, picnicking, and camping. (Photograph courtesy Holliday Lake SP.)

PRINCE EDWARD AND GOODWIN LAKES.
Camp Gallion was one of the few
African American CCC groups in the
commonwealth. This camp built the
trails and the two dams that created
the Goodwin Lake and Prince Edward
Lake Recreation Areas. These areas
were similar to Bear Creek and Holliday
Lakes. Prince Edward was developed for
recreational use by African Americans.
(Photograph courtesy Twin Lakes SP.)

PRINCE EDWARD STATE PARK. In
1948, Maceo Conrad Martin was
denied admission to Staunton River
State Park because of his race. Martin
filed suit against the commonwealth,
and this led to the expansion of the
existing recreation area for African
Americans in Prince Edward County.
In 1949, Gov. William M. Tuck wrote
an appropriation totaling $195,000
for development of the new Prince
Edward State Park for Negroes.
(Photograph courtesy Twin Lakes SP.)

PRINCE EDWARD STATE PARK
(FOR NEGROES)

LOCATION

Prince Edward State Park, exclusively for
Negroes, is located in Prince Edward County,
five miles south of Burkeville and one and one
half miles off United States Route 360. Mailing
address: Route 2, Box 93, Burkeville, Virginia.

DESCRIPTION

The park is situated in the heart of Prince Edward State Forest, and the large lake, with its white sand beach surrounded by the dark green of the forest, creates a scene of peaceful beauty and quiet. Six cabins, completely equipped for housekeeping, overlook the lake. A modern bathhouse, sandy beach, diving tower, parking area, and the picnic ground with its tables, ovens and shelter, provide comfortable facilities for large and small groups. There is a restaurant, and also a small store from which supplies may be purchased. The thirty-acre lake is well stocked with bass, crappie and bream, and boats are for

PRINCE EDWARD CABINS. The new and expanded park facilities included an enlarged swimming area, expanded parking lots, new roads, six housekeeping cabins, a bathhouse, and a concession area. (Photograph courtesy Twin Lakes SP.)

SWIMMING AREA. Although the park was never formally advertised in papers or magazines, word of mouth of the park's facilities and staff drew African American families from throughout Virginia and North Carolina. It was known by many as the family playground, where families, churches, fraternities, sororities, and other groups came to share and enjoy good food, great company, and memorable times. (Photograph courtesy VSP Collection.)

GOODWIN LAKE. Adjacent to Prince Edward State Park for Negroes was the "whites only" Goodwin Lake with its beach and picnic area. Occasionally, the two staffs would work together on large-scale projects such as updating the parks' water systems. One shared task was assisting each other in maintaining the segregation laws. Staff would be positioned on the trails to ensure that guests would stay on their respective sides. (Photograph courtesy VSP Collection.)

STATE *Recreational* AREAS

These areas were developed mainly for day use by people living within easy touring radius. None has cabins or overnight accommodations. They are open seven days a week from the last week in May through the week after Labor Day. Admittance is free to the public and there is no parking fee.

Each area has a lake, well stocked with game fish, including bass, bream and crappie. Fishing season is June 20-Nov. 30 and fishermen are required to

have either a county or a State fishing license. Each area has a bathhouse, for the use of which there is a moderate charge. In addition, each has a sand bathing beach and life guard protection. In addition, each has picnic areas with shelters, tables, drinking water, open fireplaces and sanitary facilities, all free of charge. Each also has a store where soft drinks, candies, etc., may be obtained, but these concessions do not provide prepared meals.

The beach at Goodwyn Lake.

Boating and bathing at Bear Creek Lake.

TWIN LAKES STATE PARK. The 1964 Civil Rights Act ended segregation. The two parks operated independently until 1976 and were united as Twin Lakes State Park in 1986. Retired park manager Herbert Doswell stated it well, "Twin Lakes is a representation of Virginia's culture, and in a sense, any history of a culture is a lesson in itself. Here we can all learn that forced segregation is not something to repeat." (Photograph courtesy DCR.)

AYERS FAMILY. In the 1880s, Southwest Virginia experienced an iron and coal boom that fueled the nation's industrial revolution. This led to Big Stone Gap being touted in Northern papers as the new "Pittsburgh of the South." Rufus Ayers served as Virginia's attorney general and was instrumental in the "boom" of Southwest Virginia. (Photograph courtesy Southwest Virginia Museum HSP.)

AYERS HOUSE DURING THE BOOM. The home was begun in 1888 and completed in 1895 at a cost of $25,000. The sandstone and limestone exterior was quarried locally and hand-chiseled. Native red oak was used throughout the interior with hand-carved motifs adorning the windows and doors. A unique feature of the structure is its quarter-inch, hand-sawn, tongue-and-groove flooring. (Photograph courtesy Southwest Virginia Museum HSP.)

C. BASCOM SLEMP. The Ayers house was purchased by C. Bascom Slemp in 1929. Slemp served multiple terms in Congress and became the private secretary to Pres. Calvin Coolidge. Slemp and his sister Janie Slemp Newman collected and preserved the region's material culture. It was their desire to see a museum established depicting the history of Southwest Virginia. (Photograph courtesy Southwest Virginia Museum HSP.)

SOUTHWEST VIRGINIA MUSEUM. Shortly before his death in 1943, C. Bascom Slemp established a foundation. In 1946, the commonwealth acquired the Ayers home from Slemp's estate and The Slemp Foundation donated the historical collection. The Southwest Virginia Museum Historical State Park was officially dedicated on May 30, 1948. (Photograph courtesy Southwest Virginia Museum HSP.)

MUSEUM TOUR. Exhibits tell the story of the exploration and development of Southwest Virginia from the pioneer era of the 1700s to the boom-and-bust mining era of the late 1800s. The collection includes over 25,000 pieces and state-of-the-art interpretive exhibits. Additionally, the site offers interpretive and special events, a rental cabin, and facilities for meetings, weddings, and other special occasions. (Photograph courtesy Southwest Virginia Museum HSP.)

RECREATION DEMONSTRATION AREA. This National Park Service program operated during the 1930s and 1940s, building 46 public parks near urban areas in 24 states. The NPS used Civilian Conservation Corps labor to build Recreation Demonstration Areas. Swift Creek Recreation Area was opened near Richmond on July 2, 1938. (Photograph courtesy LVA.)

CIVILIAN CONSERVATION CORPS. The first company to report for construction of Swift Creek arrived in 1935. The company was CCC 2201-VC and was comprised of World War I and Spanish-American War veterans. National Park Service reports stated that they were "physically unable to do the hard heave work required." They were replaced by much younger men in Company 2386 and Company 2364. (Photograph courtesy Pocahontas SP.)

DINING HALL. Swift Creek Recreation Area was designed to accommodate the large urban populations that were found in Richmond and Petersburg. Swift Creek was organized in clusters of various sized primitive cabins around a centrally located dining hall to accommodate large groups such as youth, church, and scout groups. (Photograph courtesy LVA.)

SWIMMING BEACH. Swift Creek was open to the public until 1942 when it was closed to be used as a recreation area for members of the military. In 1946, the ownership of Swift Creek Recreational Demonstration Area transferred from the National Park Service to the Commonwealth of Virginia. The park's name was changed shortly thereafter. (Photograph courtesy VSP Collection.)

POCAHONTAS STATE PARK. The name "Pocahontas" was selected from contest entries submitted by Chesterfield County High School seniors. The winner, Nancy Roberts, was awarded a $25 war bond. She submitted the name to honor "the young Indian princess who saved Capt. John Smith's life" and because "the future of our country was born in this county." Approximately 8,000 acres in size, Pocahontas is Virginia's largest state park. (Photograph courtesy VSP Collection.)

Four

Virginia Expands Our "Common Wealth" in the 1950s and 1960s

CLAYTOR LAKE STATE PARK. In 1946, Governor Tuck, other state officials, and citizens met to promote the idea of a new state park. Officials toured the lake and enjoyed a barbecue at the home of R. G. Stevens, an avid supporter of the proposed park. In 1947, bills were approved in the Virginia House and Senate to establish the park, with $10,000 appropriated for the project. (Photograph courtesy LVA.)

LAKESHORE RECREATION. In 1947, Appalachian Power Company donated 320 acres of land, stipulating that an adjacent 117 acres would be acquired. Dan Howe owned the acreage and agreed to sell it for $30,000. Stevens, C. E. Richardson, and Judge John S. Draper led a drive to raise funds for this purchase. An additional 35 acres were purchased in 1954, bringing the total to 472 acres. (Photograph courtesy LVA.)

DIVING. At the dedication on May 29, 1948, Governor Tuck addressed the crowd: "Claytor Lake State Park, bordering this beautiful body of water and comprising 438 acres, will constitute a most fitting addition to the chain of parks already under the supervision of the State Conservation Commission. . . . It is a prime obligation of all governments to afford the opportunity to their citizens of enjoying the blessings of life within their reach." (Photograph courtesy LVA.)

DOCK. Unfortunately, the state had no funds to operate the new park, so R. G. Stevens volunteered to become ex-officio state park superintendent. He operated the park for the committee during the 1949 and 1950 vacation seasons. Facilities at that time consisted of a small picnic area, a makeshift bathing beach, and a boat dock. (Photograph courtesy LVA.)

CABINS. The park's first paid superintendent, Ben H. Bolen, who later became commissioner of state parks, took charge on September 1, 1950. Under Bolen's leadership, the park grew rapidly. Twelve housekeeping cabins opened in 1951. The bathing beach and bathhouse were opened in 1954. Campgrounds, picnic shelters, and hiking trails soon followed. Today Claytor Lake State Park offers a wide range of recreational opportunities. (Photograph courtesy Claytor Lake SP.)

BREAKS INTERSTATE PARK.
Established in 1954, the park is administered as an "interstate park" by both Virginia and Kentucky; it is only one of three interstate parks in the nation. Often referred to as the "Grand Canyon of the South," Breaks is the deepest canyon east of the Mississippi. Along with breathtaking scenery, the park features a campground, lake, lodge, restaurant, swimming pool, cabins, and trails. (Photograph courtesy LVA.)

STAUNTON RIVER BATTLEFIELD. During the Civil War, the Army of Northern Virginia depended heavily on the Richmond-to-Danville Railroad for supplies and equipment. Defensive positions were constructed along the line to protect important structures. Fort Hill and its earthworks were established to protect the large bridge and two smaller bridges that carried the Richmond-to-Danville Railroad over the Staunton River. (Photograph courtesy Staunton River Battlefield SP.)

KAUTZ AND WILSON. Union general Ulysses S. Grant planned to destroy the tracks and the bridge. The raid, led by Brigadier Generals August V. Kautz and James H. Wilson, began on June 22, 1864. They left Petersburg with over 5,000 cavalry and 16 pieces of artillery. As they moved west, the raiders were closely pursued by Confederate general W. H. F. "Rooney" Lee and his cavalry. (Photographs courtesy the Library of Congress.)

THE BRIDGE. Some 296 Confederates under Capt. Benjamin Farinholt stood ready to defend the bridge. Farinholt later wrote, "On the 23rd, I sent off orderlies . . . urging the citizens of Halifax, Charlotte, and Mecklenburg to assemble for the defense of the bridge. . . . On the 25th, I had received, citizens and soldiers . . . 642 in re-enforcement." The 492 citizens of this old men and young boys brigade distinguished themselves, and an important supply line was protected. (Photograph courtesy Staunton River Battlefield SP.)

MULBERRY HILL PLANTATION. The home is located on a hill near the battlefield. Its grounds served as the Union headquarters and field hospital during the battle. It is said that Mrs. McPhail, lady of the house, told the Federals that 10,000 Confederates lay in wait for them beyond the breastworks and that every train was bringing more. The plantation dates to the mid-1700s. (Photograph courtesy Staunton River Battlefield SP.)

TRAIL DEDICATION. In 1955, the Fort Hill portion of the battlefield was transferred to the state. The site became Staunton River Battlefield State Park in 1995. It expanded to over 300 acres through partnerships with Old Dominion Electric Cooperative and Virginia Power, which donated land and built a visitor center; Norfolk Southern, which donated the bridge and railroad bed; and the Butler family, which donated Mulberry Hill. (Photograph courtesy Staunton River Battlefield SP.)

VIEW FROM GRAYSON. Originally named Mount Rogers State Park, Grayson Highlands State Park was established in 1965. Its name changed in 1975 due to the confusion it caused; visitors assumed that it was located on the summit of nearby Mount Rogers. The Grayson Highlands name came from state senator William Grayson and the park's mountainous "highlands" location in Grayson County. (Photograph courtesy Grayson Highlands SP.)

INSIDE COX VISITOR CENTER. Dr. Virgil Cox, a Galax physician, strongly supported the park's establishment due to his love of the outdoors, hunting, and fishing. He ran for public office and made the park his main focus during his two terms in the Virginia House of Delegates. Along with those of commissioner Ben Bolen, Cox's personal vision and hard work made Grayson a reality. (Photograph courtesy Grayson Highlands SP.)

WILD PONIES. The park features high meadows where wild ponies roam. Introduced in 1974, the ponies help maintain the "bald" areas of Grayson Highlands and Mount Rogers. The Wilburn Ridge Pony Association maintains the herd. The association patrols the herd monthly and attends to sick ponies. Ponies are auctioned at the park's fall festival to keep the herd at a sustainable level. (Photograph courtesy Grayson Highlands SP.)

PIONEER CABIN. The area was originally settled by people of Scots-Irish and German descent who lived off the land. Massie Gap takes its name from Lee Massey, who lived in the gap with his wife and five children in the late 1800s. Wilburn Ridge is named after Wilburn Waters; his reputation as a bear hunter and wolf trapper made him renowned throughout the region. (Photograph courtesy Grayson Highlands SP.)

MUSIC FESTIVAL.
Visitors to Grayson
Highlands State Park
can enjoy hiking,
camping, trout fishing,
horseback riding,
blueberry gathering,
and wild pony
watching. The park
also hosts events that
celebrate the culture of
the area. The Wayne
C. Henderson Music
Festival and Guitar
Competition occur in
June, and the Grayson
Highlands Fall Festival
is held annually
during the last full
weekend in September.
(Photograph courtesy
Grayson Highlands SP.)

SMITH MOUNTAIN LAKE. Appalachian Power completed construction in 1966 of a dam in Smith
Gap, creating the second-largest lake in Virginia, Smith Mountain Lake. The power company
donated the first parcels of land for a state park beginning in 1967. The rest of the 1,248 acres was
purchased over the next six years. (Photograph courtesy Smith Mountain Lake SP.)

PARK DEDICATION. Construction on Smith Mountain Lake Park began with the first access roads in 1975. From 1978 to 1983, several public facilities were built. They included a contact station, boat launch, restrooms, picnic area, and visitor center. The park opened to the public on July 15, 1983. (Photograph courtesy Smith Mountain Lake SP.)

LAKE FUN. Park facilities were expanded to meet growing visitor needs. Campsites were built, and electrical hookups were added later. In 1989, the park opened the first public swimming area along its 500 miles of shoreline. The 1992 bond funded cabins and the expansion of the visitor center. Twenty cabins, the first built in the system since the 1950s, were opened in 1999. (Photograph courtesy Smith Mountain Lake SP.)

CHILDREN IN NATURE. Volunteers are an integral part of the Virginia State Park System. Smith Mountain Lake State Park volunteers help staff the park's Discovery Center and assist in presenting various activities centered on the theme of "Children in Nature." They work to increase awareness of the great outdoors as well as encourage a love of nature in young and old alike. (Photograph courtesy Smith Mountain Lake SP.)

OUTDOOR RECREATION AREA DEDICATION. In 2008, the park honored delegate Victor Thomas by dedicating the beach peninsula as the A. Victor Thomas Outdoor Recreation Area. Thomas played a key role in securing funds to improve facilities at Smith Mountain Lake State Park, as well as advocating for natural resources and outdoor recreation opportunities throughout the commonwealth. (Photograph courtesy Smith Mountain Lake SP.)

Looking Down Into Natural Tunnel, Va.

NATURAL TUNNEL "EIGHTH WONDER OF THE WORLD." The 850-foot-long tunnel was nicknamed "the Eighth Wonder of the World" by famous U.S. statesman William Jennings Bryan. The tunnel is a premier feature in Southwest Virginia, an area known for its caves, sinkholes, and karst topography. (Postcard courtesy CF and Deborah Wright.)

TRAIN APPROACHES TUNNEL. Railroad tracks were laid through the tunnel in 1893. The first train, operated by the Virginia and Southwestern Railway Company, passed through the following year. In 1899, the route was purchased by the Tennessee and Carolina Iron and Steel Company. The railway originally carried passenger trains. Today a major coal-hauling line operated by Norfolk Southern Railroad runs through Natural Tunnel. (Postcard courtesy VSP Collection.)

TUNNEL PAVILION. When the pavilion was built at the mouth of the tunnel in 1906, guests could ride the Lonesome Pine Special from Bristol and enjoy a variety of recreational activities at the tunnel. The south portal pavilion became the party place for dances and galas. (Postcard courtesy VSP Collection.)

"BOWLING" CAVE POSTCARD, c. 1900. Natural Tunnel and its surrounding caverns have always attracted visitors. The original name of the cave was probably "Bowlin," but the spelling was changed over time. Signatures located in Bowling Cave date back to the early 1800s. The caves of Natural Tunnel State Park are now considered to be educational resources and are protected by the state. (Postcard courtesy C. F. and Deborah Wright.)

Dining Room - Natural Tunnel Lodge - Natural Tunnel, Va.   3-C-156

NATURAL TUNNEL LODGE. Originally, the facility was a private venture known as Natural Tunnel Chasms and Caverns Corporation. The attraction featured a lodge, gift shop, and picnic area. In 1967, the state purchased 140 acres from the corporation; Natural Tunnel State Park opened in 1971. Today the park features a visitor center, campgrounds, cabins, trails, chairlift, swimming pool, picnic area, amphitheater, education center, and . . . the Natural Tunnel. (Postcard courtesy Brenda Smith.)

BELMONT BAY. Mason Neck State Park is located on a peninsula created by the Potomac River, Belmont Bay, Pohick Bay, and Occoquan Bay. The park takes its name from George Mason IV, author of the Virginia Declaration of Rights, who owned much of the land on the peninsula. Mason's son George Mason V also lived on a plantation that fell within the boundaries of the modern state park. (Photograph courtesy VSP Collection.)

MASON NECK VISITOR CENTER. In 1965, a dozen individuals formed the Citizens' Conservation Committee in response to proposed development of the Mason Neck area. The committee wanted officials to set land aside for wildlife conservation, especially for bald eagle habitat. Their efforts led to 5,100 acres of land being protected from development. It was purchased by several separate agencies for parks and refuges. (Photograph courtesy VSP Collection.)

KANES CREEK. Mason Neck State Park opened to the public in 1985. Visitors may rent canoes and kayaks to explore Kanes Creek and look for some of the 50 bald eagles known to live and breed in the area. Wintertime brings more eagles and thousands of waterfowl to the bay, from graceful tundra swans to comical hooded mergansers, canvasbacks, buffleheads, and many more. (Photograph courtesy VSP Collection.)

MASON NECK CANOES. A day-use park, Mason Neck has become nationally known for its bald eagles and as a quiet retreat in the busy Washington, D.C., metropolitan area. The park offers activities such as hiking, bicycling, canoeing, wildlife watching, fishing, and picnicking. One of the park's main attractions is the broad range of habitats that its visitors can explore. (Photograph courtesy Mason Neck SP.)

ELIZABETH HARTWELL ENVIRONMENTAL CENTER. The park's center is named for Elizabeth Hartwell. She was one of the original 12 committee members to advocate protecting the Mason Neck and became known as "the eagle lady." The center has rotating exhibits on local wildlife and the area's history. It provides an opportunity for teachers to conduct environmental studies in a natural setting. (Photograph courtesy Mason Neck SP.)

CHIPPOKES ON THE JAMES. The area of Chippokes Plantation was Quiyoughancock Indian territory; they were led by Chief Chippokes. The plantation is across the river from Jamestown Island. It is documented that before the English settlers landed there, they landed on the Surry side of the river and were welcomed by the chief. Farmed since 1619, it is one of the oldest continually farmed plantations in the country. (Photograph courtesy Chippokes Plantation SP.)

CHIPPOKES MANSION. William Powell received the first patent for the land. The plantation changed hands many times; all of the landowners were absentees, except Albert Carroll Jones (1837–1882) and Victor and Evelyn Stewart (1918–1967). Albert Jones built the mansion that today houses an extensive antique collection. Six acres of formal gardens feature some of the oldest crepe myrtles in Virginia. (Photograph courtesy LVA.)

FARMING. Chippokes Plantation's first cash crop was tobacco. Similar to other Colonial plantations, Chippokes had slaves. In the 1800s, the plantation converted to mainly orchards. In the 1900s, the Stewarts kept dairy cows at Chippokes. In modern times, the plantation has grown milo, corn, wheat, cotton, and peanuts. Today in addition to these crops, beef cattle are raised on the plantation. (Photograph courtesy VSP Collection.)

TENANT FARMERS. After emancipation, many African American families farmed Chippokes as sharecroppers and tenant farmers. Descendents of these early African Americans have been instrumental in preserving Chippokes as a state park. (Photograph courtesy Chippokes Plantation SP.)

EVELYN STEWART. Victor and Evelyn Stewart purchased the property in 1918. By 1935, the plantation was fully operational and restored to excellent condition. Victor Stewart died in 1965. In 1967, Evelyn Stewart donated the property in honor of her late husband. She required that the land continue to remain a working plantation, and thus, Chippokes Plantation State Park was born. (Photograph courtesy Chippokes Plantation SP.)

FALSE CAPE. The cape is a mile-wide barrier spit between the Back Bay and the Atlantic Ocean in eastern Virginia. False Cape got its name because its land mass resembled Cape Henry, confusing sailors into piloting their boats into treacherously shallow waters. In the 1800s, False Cape gained a reputation as a ship's graveyard. (Photograph courtesy VSP Collection.)

WASH WOODS CHURCH. One of False Cape's first communities, Wash Woods, was developed by survivors of a shipwreck. At the center of this community was the Wash Woods Methodist Church. The church was built from an 1895 shipwreck loaded with cypress lumber. The community even had its own voting precinct and was the first in the commonwealth to report results each year. (Photograph courtesy VSP Collection.)

HUNT CLUBS. Just before the turn of the 20th century, hunters began forming clubs. For a number of years, False Cape became a haven for prestigious hunt clubs, which took advantage of the area's abundance of waterfowl. These clubs often hired locals to be caretakers of the buildings and grounds. Today one of the old club buildings is used as the Wash Woods Environmental Education Center. (Photograph courtesy VSP Collection.)

WASH WOODS CEMETERY. Wash Woods was home to a Coast Guard station, grocery store, two churches, a cemetery, and a school. Some 300 people once lived there, working as fishermen, farmers, hunting guides, and manning lifeboats. Due to the storms, the difficult lifestyle, and villages being buried by sand, many of the residents began to move. A mass exodus from Wash Woods occurred in the late 1920s. (Photograph courtesy VSP Collection.)

FALSE CAPE STATE PARK. The state purchased 4,300 acres in 1968, after the recommendation of the 1965 outdoors study. Today the park is one of the last undisturbed coastal environments on the East Coast. Vehicles are prohibited in the park; visitors must either hike, bike, or canoe into the park. Special rides on the Terra Gator and tram are available at certain times of the year. (Photograph courtesy VSP Collection.)

OCCONEECHEE PLANTATION. The park name originates with the Occoneechi people who lived on an island in the Roanoke River. In 1760, Thomas Jefferson's uncle Field Jefferson owned the 2,200-acre Occoneechee Farm on the park site. William Townes built the Occoneechee Plantation house in 1839. Only the remnants of the terrace garden with its enormous boxwoods and Osage orange trees can still be seen. (Photograph courtesy Occoneechee SP.)

BUGGS ISLAND LAKE, 1961. Native Americans called the Roanoke the "river of death" due to flooding. Plans were made as early as the 1920s to dam the river at Buggs Island in Mecklenburg County. Construction took from 1946 until 1953 and cost $92 million. When the 50,000-acre reservoir was completed, the three islands inhabited by the Occoneechi were lost below the waters of the lake. (Photograph courtesy Occoneechee SP.)

BOAT DOCK, 1950s. A proposal in the 1966 outdoor recreation plan was "a site on the northern shore of Buggs Island Lake with good access from major roads deserves high priority as a state park." The Army Corps of Engineers developed the original master plan for Occoneechee Park. From 1962 to 1968, the Buggs Island Park Authority, formed by Mecklenburg County, managed the park. (Photograph courtesy Occoneechee SP.)

FUELING FLORRIE, 1950s. Virginia assumed management of Occoneechee on July 1, 1968, by a renewable lease with the Army Corps of Engineers. The corps' original master plan focused the park on the Clarksville Regatta, which was at the height of its popularity. It included expanded boat launches, boat maintenance facilities, a boat storage building, bleachers overlooking the lake, and a raised earthen mound for boat display. (Photograph courtesy Occoneechee SP.)

OCCONEECHEE STATE PARK CAMPGROUND, 1961. Original facilities included three campgrounds with 96 campsites, a boat launch area with a marina and fuel sales, picnic areas with shelters, and hiking trails. Today the park has significantly expanded and upgraded these facilities, having added a visitor center, amphitheater, and cabins. Every year, tribal members host the Occoneechee Powwow at the park. (Photograph courtesy Occoneechee SP.)

YORK RIVER STATE PARK AERIAL. This area, where freshwater and saltwater meet to create an estuary habitat, was a center for early native people. English colonists found Mattaponi and Pumunkey Indians inhabiting the peninsula. Many of the trails and landmarks in the park are named to reflect this rich history, including Taskinas Creek and Mattaponi, Pumunkey, and Powhatan Forks Trails. (Photograph courtesy VSP Collection.)

TASKINAS CREEK. During the 1600s, a tobacco inspection wharf existed between the mouth of Taskinas Creek and another nearby smaller creek. During the 1700s, large plantations lined the shores of the York River. Three plantations existed in or slightly outside of present-day park boundaries; two were built on Taskinas Creek. John Blair Jr., one of the three Virginia signers of the Constitution, owned Taskinas Plantation. (Photograph courtesy VSP Collection.)

CROAKER LANDING. During the 19th and 20th centuries, the land passed through a variety of owners. In 1969, the state purchased 2,507 acres to develop York River State Park. The site has many natural and historic features. An area around Croaker Landing has been identified as a former Native American encampment and is an archaeological site included in the National Register of Historic Places. (Photograph courtesy VSP Collection.)

CANOEING ON TASKINAS CREEK. Taskinas Creek and the surrounding watershed is a Chesapeake Bay National Estuarine Research Reserve. Visitors experience salt marsh ecology on the canoe trip. Taskinas Creek begins as freshwater wetlands and then gradually turns into a deeper tidal creek before it joins the York River. A fun aspect of the trip is getting to see tiny fiddler crabs close-up. (Photograph courtesy VSP Collection.)

CROAKER LANDING PIER. York River State Park encompasses 2,554 acres of land. It features over 3 miles of waterfront, 25 miles of trails, picnic areas with shelters, and playgrounds. Croaker Landing features a boat launch and a 360-foot fishing pier, which was funded through various partnerships. The landing is a great place to catch catfish, spot, striper, and croaker. (Photograph courtesy DCR.)

Five

CONSERVATION AND RECREATION IN THE 1970s AND 1980s

LAKE ANNA GOLD MINING. Before the California Gold Rush, Virginia was the nation's third-leading gold producer from 1830 to 1849. The Goodwin Mineshaft, located on Pigeon Creek within Lake Anna State Park, was 95 feet deep and 200 feet into the hillside. Tours of the mine site and panning for gold are popular historical programs at the park. (Photograph courtesy DCR.)

MINE STEAM ENGINE. Early mining was accomplished manually, using pans, rocker boxes, and toms to process stream sediment to find gold. By the 1870s, mine shafts were dug and steam engines were used to power rock-crushing machinery. The rock dust was then processed to remove the gold. (Photograph courtesy Lake Anna SP.)

GLENORA. The house was built by Scottish businessman John Jerdone around 1832; the plantation quickly grew to 3,000 acres. In 1860, with the approach of the Civil War, Jerdone sold the home. Over the next century, various people owned the land until the park's establishment. For safety reasons, the house was torn down. The site's smokehouse was renovated using original boards from the house. (Photograph courtesy Lake Anna SP.)

LAKE ANNA STATE PARK. Construction on Lake Anna began in 1967. The lake basin was cleared to dam the North Anna River to supply cooling water for a nuclear power plant. In January 1972, the dam gates were closed and the basin filled within the year. Shortly thereafter, 2,032 acres with 8.5 miles of shoreline were acquired to develop Lake Anna State Park. (Photograph courtesy DCR.)

LAKE ANNA PONTOON BOAT. The original park plan called for a campground, swimming beach, boat launch, trails, and a visitor center. Delays in funding and construction kept the park from officially opening until 1982. The park offers camping, cabins, trails, picnic areas, a visitor center, swimming beach, playground, boat ramp, and interpretive rides on a pontoon boat. (Photograph courtesy Lake Anna SP.)

CALEDON CARETAKER'S HOUSE. John and Phillip Alexander, founders of Alexandria, purchased 1,500 acres on the Potomac in 1659. They named the property Salisbury, and their house was called Caledon. The land was divided as it passed through generations. In the late 1800s, William Smoot inherited part of the property, which was known by that time as Caledon. This 1850s house is the oldest structure at Caledon. (Photograph courtesy Caledon.)

STUART'S WHARF, c. 1910. This steamship landing was located at Caledon. The tragic 1873 fire on the *Wawaset* steamship happened upriver from the wharf. Many bodies were pulled out of the river and placed on the wharf dock for the coroner's inquest. Boats carrying family members and the press docked at Stuart's Wharf for people to make their way along the Potomac shore to identify bodies. (Photograph courtesy Caledon.)

SMOOT HOUSE. In 1974, Gov. Mills E. Godwin accepted the donation of 2,529 acres from Ann Hopewell Smoot to be developed and managed as a state park. Smoot stated in the local papers, "By donating it (Caledon) to the commonwealth, the natural beauty as well as the historical importance will be forever preserved." The Smoot House serves as Caledon's Visitor Center. (Photograph courtesy Caledon.)

CALEDON NATURAL AREA. In 1981, conservationists from the Chesapeake Bay area expressed concerns about developing Caledon. In 1982, the Caledon Natural Area Task Force was appointed by Gov. Chuck Robb. After several meetings, the task force recommended in 1984 to make Caledon a natural area. Shortly thereafter, Governor Robb made the designation official. Caledon's trails, visitor center, and grounds were opened to the public on May 17, 1986. (Photograph courtesy Caledon.)

BIRD WATCHING. Records reveal that Caledon has been prime eagle habitat for hundreds of years. The site is an awe-inspiring opportunity to observe an American bald eagle in its habitat along the Potomac River. Visitors may see an eagle soaring over the river or perched along the shoreline on ranger-guided tours. (Photograph courtesy DCR.)

SKY MEADOW'S MOUNT BLEAK. The centerpiece of Sky Meadows State Park, located in the Shenandoah Valley, is the 1840s home built by Abner and Mary Settle. The house sits on a prominent ridge from which the Settles and their 12 children could view the surrounding countryside. In naming their new home Mount Bleak, the Settles used the term *bleak* as it was defined in the early 1900s, when it commonly meant "exposed or breezy." (Photograph courtesy DCR.)

Mosby's Rangers. When the Civil War came to the valley, most families were torn both physically and emotionally. Abner Settle's son Thomas Lee volunteered to join the 7th Virginia Cavalry as an army surgeon, and two other sons—Isaac Morgan and Abner Carroll—decided to protect their hearth and homes by joining in the independent command of Col. John S. Mosby. (Photograph courtesy Sky Meadows SP.)

Antebellum Life Reenacted. Though all three sons returned home safe and sound, by the end of the Civil War, the Settles were in ill health and financially strapped. In 1866, Abner and Mary sold Mount Bleak and moved to Delaplane, then known as Piedmont Station. (Photograph courtesy DCR.)

SKY MEADOWS. During World War II, British consul general Robert Hadow and his family would spend summers on the property. Mount Bleak reminded him so much of Scotland's Isle of Skye that he christened the property Skye Farm. In 1949, Mount Bleak–resident U.S. attorney general John Scott used the name Sky Meadows. (Photograph courtesy DCR.)

SKY MEADOWS STATE PARK. In the 1970s, Fauquier County was slated for development around the Crooked Run Valley and Ashby's Gap area. Paul Mellon wanted to preserve the land, and in 1973, he obtained the deed to the 1,132-acre Mount Bleak farm. Mellon donated the farm for the park in 1975. After preparation of trails and other facilities, the park was opened in 1983. (Photograph courtesy DCR.)

FREESTONE POINT. The area of Leesylvania State Park was called Freestone Point. The name comes from the land's sandstone, which was of such poor quality that it was given away for free to local builders. In 1608, Capt. John Smith sailed the Potomac past Freestone Point on his way to the Occoquan River. He described the area as heavily forested and the river as teeming with fish. (Photograph courtesy Leesylvania SP.)

LEE MONUMENT. The land was acquired by Laetitia and Richard Lee II in the 1600s. Their youngest son, Henry Lee, inherited the land and passed it to his youngest son, Henry Lee II. This Lee established his plantation around 1754, naming it Leesylvania, which means "Lee's woods." It was the boyhood home of Henry Lee III, better known as Revolutionary War hero "Light Horse Harry" Lee. (Photograph courtesy Leesylvania SP.)

FAIRFAX CHIMNEY. The Lee family home burned in the 1790s, and in 1825, the land was sold to Henry Fairfax for the sum of $9,600. His son John, later an aide to Confederate general James Longstreet, inherited the property in 1847. The Fairfax house burned in 1910, but many remnants remain on the site, including a large chimney that has been restored. (Photograph courtesy Leesylvania SP.)

LEESYLVANIA STATE PARK EXHIBITS. Robert E. Lee requested the use of his father's ancestral home for a Confederate cannon battery to prevent Union ships from reaching Washington, D.C. On September 25, 1861, the battery of Freestone Point was fired upon by the Union flotilla. It is believed that Fairfax's slaves swam out to the passing ships to warn them about the battery. (Photograph courtesy DCR.)

GOV. BOB McDONNELL PLANTS TREE AT LEESYLVANIA. In the 1970s, property owner Daniel Ludwig offered to sell Leesylvania to the commonwealth for half of its market value for the creation of a park. Virginia acquired the land in 1978 and spent the next 11 years developing the park. On June 17, 1989, Leesylvania State Park opened to the public. (Photograph courtesy DCR.)

NEW RIVER IRON FURNACE. The village of Foster Falls, located in the New River Valley, arose from the flourishing iron industry; the falls are named after early landowner William Foster. An iron furnace was constructed there in 1881. The furnace, an open-top, cold-blast operation, was powered by water from the New River. (Photograph courtesy Hagley Museum.)

FURNACE WORKERS. The Foster Falls Mining Company processed around 2,000 pounds of pig iron per year, and at its peak, it employed 80 workers. In 1899, the furnace was sold to Virginia Iron Coal and Coke Company, which converted to a steam-powered operation, increasing its production. The mining company built over 100 company-owned homes to house furnace employees. (Photograph courtesy New River SP.)

RAILWAY LINE. In 1882, work began on the Cripple Creek Extension of the Norfolk and Western Railway. The extension ran 47 miles from Pulaski, through Foster Falls, and on to Ivanhoe. Raw iron ore was transported to the furnace from mines in Wythe County aboard narrow-gauge railroads called dinky trains. The finished product was shipped to markets in St. Louis, Baltimore, and Cincinnati. (Photograph courtesy New River SP.)

FOSTER FALLS DEPOT. By late 1890s, the village of Foster Falls boasted a number of establishments: a post office, gristmill, sawmill, general store, distillery, hotel, and a railroad depot and freight station. The station was built in 1887 on the Cripple Creek Branch and was restored by the New River Trail State Park. It currently serves as a visitor center. (Photograph courtesy New River SP.)

HOTEL. The mining company built the hotel in 1887. For 25 years, it was the community's center serving as commissary, post office, and boardinghouse. In 1914, due to flooding, the furnace ceased operations. The hotel was sold in 1919 and became a girls' industrial school. It converted into a coed orphanage in 1938; the orphanage relocated in the 1960s. (Photograph courtesy New River SP.)

SHOT TOWER. In 1805, Thomas Jackson used slave labor to construct a 75-foot tower to make shot for pioneer hunters. Lead was hoisted to the top and smelted, adding arsenic to make it pliable. It was poured into sizing sieves and fell through the tower center into water at the bottom. Acquired in 1964, the Shot Tower is now part of New River Trail State Park. (Photograph courtesy VSP Collection.)

NEW RIVER TRAIL STATE PARK. The abandoned 1800s Cripple Creek Branch of the Norfolk and Western rail line, along with a spur line, was donated in 1986 by the Norfolk and Southern Corporation. This 57-mile trail, paralleling the New River, is one of the country's most significant "rails-to-trails" facilities. It passes through historic areas, including Foster Falls, the Shot Tower, and two hydroelectric dams. (Photograph courtesy DCR.)

Six

MODERN PARKS AND
HISTORIC PATHS

KIPTOPEKE FERRY, 1950s. *Kiptopeke* is a Native American word meaning "Big Water." In the 1930s, the Virginia Ferry Corporation was chartered to provide ferry service from Virginia Beach to the town of Cape Charles on the eastern shore. In the 1940s, the corporation relocated its northern terminus, at a cost of $2.75 million, to another site, which was named Kiptopeke Beach. (Photograph courtesy Kiptopeke SP.)

PIER CONSTRUCTION, 1940s. The corporation built the pier and terminal building and platted the property for residential development. The ferry terminal was operated from 1950 until 1956. The Chesapeake Bay Ferry Commission became the governing body of the ferry passenger and freight-line services. It developed the idea of building the Chesapeake Bay Bridge Tunnel, which was opened April 1964, thus ending the ferry service to Kiptopeke. (Photograph courtesy Kiptopeke SP.)

McCLOSKEY SHIPS. As part of the ferry's development, nine McCloskey ships were partially sunk as a protective breakwater off the beach. These ships had been constructed by McCloskey and Company of Philadelphia in 1942. Each was made of concrete because of a steel shortage due to World War II. Today the ships still provide coastline protection and habitat for fish and birds. (Photograph courtesy Virginia Images Photography.)

TOURINNS POSTCARD. A 57-unit Tourinns motel and restaurant opened in January 1954 in what is today Kiptopeke State Park's picnic area. Managed by C. M. Pipher for the Kipco Corporation, it provided ferry guests with lodging until it closed in 1964 when ferry service ended. In 1989, John Maddox began developing the area into a resort campground. (Postcard courtesy VSP Collection.)

KIPTOPEKE STATE PARK. In 1992, the state acquired Maddox's campground and opened the park within 28 days of its purchase. The park is ideal for fisherman, beachgoers, and birdwatchers. Overnight guests enjoy a variety of facilities, including the only yurt in the state park system, lodges, rental trailers, and campsites. (Photograph courtesy Kiptopeke SP.)

BEL AIR AERIAL VIEW. Bel Air is a 33-acre peninsula on Deep Creek that is part of the 739-acre Belle Isle State Park in Lancaster County. The park's main property forms another peninsula bordered by Mulberry Creek, Deep Creek, and the Rappahannock River. Nearly one-third of the property is separated from the mainland by a saltwater marsh, connected only by an earthen causeway. (Photograph courtesy Belle Isle SP.)

BEL AIR MANSION. The park was part of Belle Isle Plantation. The plantation mansion, which is privately owned, was built in 1760. It was restored in the 1940s by Thomas Tilson Waterman, the first director of the American Historic Buildings Survey. This program employed architects, draftsmen, and photographers during the Great Depression. Waterman designed the Bel Air mansion while restoring the Belle Isle Plantation mansion. (Photograph courtesy Belle Isle SP.)

BEL AIR. Built in 1942, Bel Air was the home of Mr. and Mrs. John Garland Pollard Jr. This Colonial-style house was constructed using interior materials from other historic buildings in the local area. Current furnishings in the building include Colonial reproduction furniture and Oriental rugs that maintain the structure's historic character. Bel Air mansion is available for rent by the public. (Photograph courtesy Belle Isle SP.)

MULBERRY CREEK DOCK. Studies indicated that the Northern Neck on the Chesapeake Bay was rapidly losing its undeveloped waterfront. The search for park sites began in 1989. The parkland was purchased through a 1992 bond referendum, and the park opened in 1994. There are eight distinct types of wetlands within the park, which makes Belle Isle an excellent outdoor laboratory for environmental education. (Photograph courtesy DCR.)

BAY SEAFOOD FESTIVAL. Several thousand visitors attend the annual Bay Seafood Festival at Belle Isle State Park. Organized by the area Rotary club, this all-you-can-eat event features numerous varieties of fresh seafood from Virginia's coastal waters. The festival is one example of the many special events held at state parks across Virginia. (Photograph courtesy DCR.)

JAMES RIVER TUBING. James River State Park is located on the middle James River, where visitors recreate and relax on this historic route. Native Americans first used the river as a trading route. Europeans arrived by way of the river, built homes, and planted the fertile river bottoms. In the 1700s, the Cabell family built a plantation known as Green Hill within today's park boundaries. (Photograph courtesy DCR.)

BATEAU ON THE JAMES. Plantation owners along the James River needed to transport tobacco to Richmond efficiently. A large flat-bottomed boat, called a bateau, was invented around 1770 by a local planter, Samual Rucker. It could carry large cargo, drafting only inches in the water, which allowed the boat to float over ledges and rocks. Bateau boat heritage is celebrated at an annual festival on the James River. (Photograph courtesy DCR.)

TYE RIVER OVERLOOK. In 1785, work crews began digging the Kanawha Canal on the James River. When it was complete, boats, called packets, were pulled by mule or oxen along a towpath beside the canal. The route, from Richmond to the Alleghenies, would move goods from east to west and into the Ohio Valley. At the confluence of the Tye River and the James River was a canal hub town. (Photograph courtesy DCR.)

ALONG THE RIVER. The canal was bought by the Richmond and Alleghany Railroad and track laid following the towpath. Around the same period, some of the Cabell land was sold to Madison Dixon. The Dixons built a home on the old foundation of the Green Hill Plantation house and lived there for several generations. A local developer bought the land in the 1970s. (Photograph courtesy DCR.)

JAMES RIVER STATE PARK CABIN. The 1992 Bond Act made funding available to acquire a state park along the Middle James River. An initial 849-acre tract was purchased in 1993. Subsequent tracts were acquired from various landowners, bringing the total acreage to 1,557. The park opened in 1999 and features 3 miles of river frontage, three fishing ponds, overnight accommodations, and 15 miles of hiking trails. (Photograph courtesy DCR.)

ELY HOME AT WILDERNESS ROAD. Robert Ely built this Victorian home in the 1870s. Before the home was completed, he became sick and died. Ely's family was in Missouri, and he never lived to see them return. Ely descendents lived in the home until the 1940s, when it was purchased by Karl and Ann Harris. The house's exterior was changed from a Victorian to an antebellum style. (Photograph courtesy VSP Collection.)

KARLAN MANSION. The property passed to the Harrises' sons Nelson and David in the 1980s. Nelson renamed the property Karlan, which was a combination of his parents' names. In 1993, the state acquired the property and it was opened as Karlan State Park. The park's name changed to Wilderness Road State Park in 1998 to reflect the park's location on this historic path. (Photograph courtesy VSP Collection.)

RAID. In 1775, Daniel Boone cut a path westward to Cumberland Gap, the gateway to Kentucky and the Midwest, and by 1800, more than 300,000 settlers had traveled the Wilderness Road. Before Boone formally blazed the trail, several other people had already explored the area. Six years before Boone arrived, along what would become known as the Wilderness Road, Joseph Martin built a station that included cabins, a stockade, and a corn plot. However, before the corn ripened, Native Americans attacked, and the station was abandoned. (Photograph courtesy DCR.)

MARTIN'S STATION. In 1775, Martin returned to the area and built a new station on the site of the old one. As the last fortified station prior to reaching new lands in Kentucky, Martin's Station was a well-known stop for pioneers traveling the Wilderness Road. The station was reconstructed, beginning in 1992, by staff and volunteers dressed in period clothing and using historic tools and construction methods. (Photograph courtesy DCR.)

RAID AT WILDERNESS ROAD STATE PARK. The park's signature event, the "Raid on Martin's Station" reenactment, is held each May. The event features frontier militia, Cherokee warriors, an 18th-century trade fair, period workshops, and more. Similar to other partnerships in state parks, the event is supported by the park's citizen support group, Friends of Wilderness Road State Park. (Photograph courtesy DCR.)

SHENANDOAH RIVER OVERLOOK. Located in the valley between Shenandoah National Forest and Massanutten Mountain, Shenandoah River State Park affords visitors scenic mountain views and 5 acres of riverfront on the south fork of the Shenandoah. The area within this valley contains sites of some of the oldest known permanent Native American habitations in the eastern United States. (Photograph courtesy LVA.)

SHENANDOAH. It is likely that early settlers transformed an unknown Native American word into *Shenandoah*. Some believe that the word originated as the name of an Iroquoian chief; others believe that the term meant "great meadow" or "big flat place." The most popular theory holds that *Shenandoah* means "beautiful daughter of the stars." The name is attached to several landmarks, including the river, valley, town, a national park, and the 1,620-acre Shenandoah River State Park. (Photograph courtesy DCR.)

SHENANDOAH RIVER CAMPGROUND. Originally, Warren County wanted to use the property as a landfill site. It was discovered that the land was unsuitable, so it became available for the park. Multiple tracts were acquired, beginning in 1994. The official park name is the Raymond R. 'Andy' Guest Jr. Shenandoah River State Park. Guest was the Warren County delegate when the park was acquired. (Photograph courtesy DCR.)

YOUTH CONSERVATION CORPS. Shenandoah River State Park participates in the Youth Conservation Corps, a challenging developmental program for young adults. Participants assist with an assortment of projects in the Virginia State Parks, including wildlife and fisheries habitat improvement, trail and campground construction, timber and shoreline improvement, and landscape beautification. These young adults enhance their work skills while developing a volunteer, stewardship, and conservation ethic. (Photograph courtesy DCR.)

CABIN. The park features trails, campgrounds, bathhouses, a visitor center, picnic shelters, and cabins. The 2002 Bond for Virginia State Parks funded new facilities, including cabins and family lodges, camping cabins, visitor centers, campgrounds, and equestrian campgrounds. The bond funds also enabled much-needed improvements to existing facilities and infrastructure at most parks. (Photograph courtesy DCR.)

HIGH BRIDGE. The historic steel truss bridge, called High Bridge, crosses the Appomattox River. The South Side Railroad began its construction in 1849 and connected with the Richmond and Danville Railroad by 1852. This 21-span High Bridge is 2,400 feet long and reaches a height of 125 feet. It was considered the largest bridge in the world at the time of construction. (Photograph courtesy Library of Congress.)

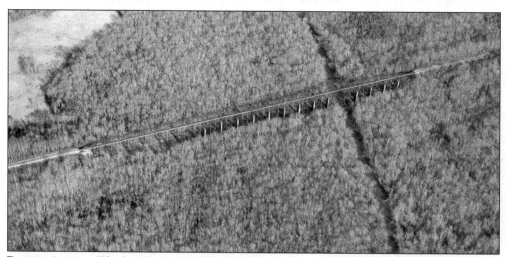

BRIDGE AERIAL. The battles for High Bridge on April 6 and 7, 1865, were significant in the final days of the Civil War. On April 6, Union troops, wanting to make High Bridge impassable, attempted to cut off Lee's retreat route to nearby Farmville, where supplies awaited him. Union losses were great, including 800 men captured, and the Confederacy kept High Bridge intact. (Photograph courtesy High Bridge SP.)

BRIDGE IN 1865. On April 7, Confederate forces retreated toward Farmville, burning four spans of High Bridge as they moved. The adjacent wagon bridge was captured by Union forces before it became fully engulfed. Because Union forces could keep advancing, Lee ordered his army's supplies shipped to Appomattox. Two days later, April 9, 1865, Lee surrendered at Appomattox Courthouse. (Photograph courtesy High Bridge SP.)

ON TOP OF HIGH BRIDGE. Between 1870 and 1901, High Bridge underwent structural changes. The brick piers received steel reinforcement, and the wooden superstructure was replaced with steel. The bridge was realigned, and a new steel truss was constructed adjacent to the old High Bridge in 1914. The last passenger train ran in 1979, and the last freight train ran in 2005. (Photograph courtesy the Library of Congress.)

HIGH BRIDGE TRAIL STATE PARK. Norfolk-Southern abandoned the line in 2005. Local leaders Sarah Puckett and Sherry Swinson and delegates Abbitt and Hogan led park establishment efforts. A donation ceremony was held in 2007 and in 2008; the first 4 miles of trail opened. In 2009, sixteen more miles were opened. In total, 30 miles of trail and the bridge will be available. (Photograph courtesy High Bridge Trail SP.)

SEVEN BENDS POSTCARD. According to the 2006 *Virginia Outdoors Survey*, the main reasons the public supports state parks are because they conserve natural resources; provide people places to explore and enjoy nature and their cultural heritage; and provide places for walking, running, and other activities that contribute to a healthy lifestyle. Parks for future development include Seven Bends, Powhatan, Widewater, Middle Peninsula, Mayo River, and Biscuit Run. (Postcard courtesy VSP Collection.)

Seven

"Virginia is for Lovers" of Parks

Will Carson. In 1885, the Irish-born Carson came to Front Royal, where his father operated a lime plant. Successful in business and Democratic politics, he managed Harry F. Byrd's 1925 gubernatorial campaign. As governor, Byrd appointed Carson chairman of the new Commission on Conservation and Development. From 1926 to 1934, Carson helped create the historical markers program, Shenandoah and Colonial National Historical Parks, and Virginia's first six state parks. (Photograph courtesy LVA.)

Park Development Sign. The Virginia State Parks overall design was linked to that of the National Park Service (NPS). The State Parks Division of the Emergency Conservation Work Act, under the NPS, oversaw the CCC's work in the parks. Landscape architects Frederick Fay (of the NPS) and R. E. Burson (of VSP) worked closely to implement the NPS Master Planning process in Virginia's first six parks. (Photograph courtesy Westmoreland SP.)

R. E. Burson at Hungry Mother. Pictured fourth from the left, with community leaders and Civilian Conservation Corps supervisors, Burson was the first VSP commissioner (director) from 1936 to 1939. A trained landscape architect, Burson developed the master plans for the first six state parks. Today one of the campgrounds at Hungry Mother State Park is named Camp Burson in his honor. (Photograph courtesy Hungry Mother SP.)

BURSON AT SEASHORE. Burson, on the left, looks across the water with Gov. Elbert Lee Trinkle. The men were well acquainted, and Trinkle was an early supporter of parks. While governor, Trinkle allocated $5,000 for roadside park acquisition, but it was removed from the budget. In 1936, as former governor, Trinkle was present to introduce Gov. George C. Peery at Hungry Mother State Park's opening ceremony. (Photograph courtesy VSP Collection.)

EARLY PARK STAFF. The first managers were called "park custodians." Some had been involved in the planning and construction of the first six parks. Later the heads of each park were called "superintendents," and today they are called "park managers." In the early years, staff members had mainly construction backgrounds. As the park system grew, professional skills in resource management, environmental education, law enforcement, construction, public relations, and business administration were required of staff members. (Photograph courtesy VSP.)

STAUNTON RIVER LIFEGUARD. From the opening of the first six parks, seasonal employees such as lifeguards, contact rangers, maintenance rangers, and program interpreters have been critical in park operations. In modern times, approximately 850 seasonal employees enhance the visitors' experience at parks across the commonwealth. Many of the parks' professional staff started their careers as seasonals and interns. (Photograph courtesy Staunton River SP.)

RANDOLPH ODELL. Commissioner Odell served from 1939 to 1961 through changing times in the country and state parks. In 1943, in response to gasoline rationing and other wartime restrictions, the Virginia Conservation Commission voted to temporarily close the parks and make their facilities available for the military. After the war, the parks reopened to face a new challenge: in 1948 and 1952, the Staunton River and Seashore State Parks' discrimination lawsuits would lead to operational changes in the park system. (Photograph courtesy DCR.)

EDGAR LATHAM. Prince Edward State Park for Negroes was opened in June 1950; it was Virginia's only pre–civil rights–era state park for African Americans. Latham, formerly a lifeguard at the Prince Edward Recreation Area, was the first African American VSP superintendent in history. Through his dedication to the park and community, Latham enhanced recreational activities and improved the quality of life for citizens in the area. (Photograph courtesy Twin Lakes SP.)

BEN BOLEN AND GOV. A. LINWOOD HOLTON. Bolen began his career as superintendent of Claytor Lake in 1950, was appointed the assistant commissioner in 1959, and served as commissioner from 1961 to 1981. The system grew dramatically during his tenure: 13 new parks were opened and six natural areas were acquired. He increased employee training, obtained police power for rangers, supported interpretive programming, and implemented the first computerized reservation system in the nation. (Photograph courtesy VSP Collection.)

SEASHORE DESIGNATED NATIONAL NATURAL LANDMARK. The Natural Landmark program recognizes and encourages the conservation of outstanding examples of America's natural history. Virginia's original six state parks, as well as numerous others, are also on the Virginia Landmarks Register and the National Register of Historic Places. These three official site lists seek to recognize the nation's historical, cultural, and natural foundations. (Photograph courtesy First Landing SP.)

TREE PLANTING. Women were actively involved in early efforts to establish and preserve parks across Virginia. Women's associations, environmental groups, and organizations such as the Virginia State Garden Club, United Daughters of the Confederacy, and Daughters of the American Revolution were instrumental in supporting parks. Pictured holding the shovel is Lynda Johnson Robb with delegate Elmon Gray to her right. (Photograph courtesy VSP Collection.)

DANETTE MCADOO. In 1984, McAdoo became the VSP's first female park superintendent. McAdoo began her career as a seasonal employee at Seashore and Pocahontas Parks in the 1970s. She would go on to serve as chief ranger/interpreter of Seashore and Caledon Parks, assistant manager at Westmoreland, and park manager at York River, False Cape, and Chippokes Plantation State Parks. (Photograph courtesy McAdoo.)

RONALD SUTTON. VSP director Ron Sutton served from 1982 to 1991 and was formerly director of the Design and Construction Section of Virginia's Department of Conservation and Recreation, as well as the VSP's assistant director. From left to right, posing at the opening of the Lake Anna State Park beach, are Sutton, Gov. Douglas Wilder, DCR secretary Elizabeth Haskell, and her husband. (Photograph courtesy Lake Anna SP.)

DENNIS BAKER. A strong advocate for interpretive programming in state parks, Baker began his career as a naturalist at Seashore State Park. He then served as the head of the Interpretive and Education Section, assistant director, and as VSP director from 1991 to 1994. (Photograph courtesy VSP Collection.)

JOE ELTON. VSP director Joe Elton holds the coveted Sports Foundation Gold Medal Award, along with NPS director Fran Mainella. The gold medal is given to the state park system considered most outstanding in recreational management and which best provides parks, recreation, and leisure services to its citizens. From 2009 to 2011, Elton served as the president of the National Association of State Park Directors. (Photograph courtesy DCR.)

VSP Directors. The woman pictured is Barbara Jackson, retired VSP executive secretary. She worked under four different VSP directors, shown here from left to right: Ben Bolen, Ron Sutton, Joe Elton, and Dennis Baker. (Photograph courtesy DCR.)

First Landing Reenactment. Virginia's parks are part of the foundation of America. As part of America's 400th Anniversary, Jamestown 2007, the settlers' landing on the site of present-day First Landing State Park was reenacted on April 26, 2007. The event featured replicas of the ships used by John Smith and the English settlers: the *Susan Constant*, *Godspeed*, and *Discovery*. (Photograph courtesy DCR.)

CHILDREN IN NATURE INITIATIVE. Pictured are VSP and NPS managers with other professional staff after meeting to discuss a new national effort. Adopted in 2007, the Children and Nature Plan for Action challenged all state and national parks to collaborate on ways to connect children and families to nature and to assist each other with programs, marketing, and resources to better serve park visitors. (Photograph courtesy DCR.)

STATE PARK OFFICERS. The agency's law enforcement program is accredited through the Virginia Law Enforcement Professional Standards Commission. Pictured from left to right are Dave Collett, District VII manager; Harvey Thompson, Grayson Highlands manager; Marceia Holland, Grayson Highlands assistant manager; and Warren Wahl, VSP assistant director. Holland received an award for graduating first in her class; she was the first female officer to attain this distinction. (Photograph courtesy DCR.)

Youth Conservation Corps Award. In 2007, Gov. Tim Kaine honored the Youth Conservation Program as the "best youth volunteer program in Virginia." In 2010, the program was named the Outstanding State Volunteer Program in the United States by the Take Pride in America program. Take Pride in America is a nationwide partnership program authorized by Congress to promote the appreciation and stewardship of the nation's public lands. (Photograph courtesy DCR.)

The Future. In his 1930 book, *Virginia Beautiful*, Wallace Nutting wrote of Will Carson's efforts to preserve Virginia: "Sometimes we hesitate to provide far enough in the future . . . years from now the grandchildren will bless us for every square mile thus forever secured." Generations, both past and present, benefit from the efforts to create and conserve Virginia's state parks. (Photograph courtesy DCR.)

BIBLIOGRAPHY

Byrne, John. *The Civilian Conservation Corps In Virginia, 1933–1942*. University of Montana, 1982.

Department of Conservation and Recreation, *A Natural Legacy*. 1992.

Department of Conservation and Recreation, *Virginia's Common Wealth*. 1965.

Department of Conservation and Recreation, *Virginia Outdoor Plan*. 2007.

Horan, John. *Will Carson and The Virginia Conservation Commission, 1926–1934*. University of North Carolina, Department of History, 1977.

Land and Community Associates. *Survey of State Owned Properties, Division of Parks*. Department of Conservation and Recreation, 1988.

Lotspeich, Stephen. *The Design Intentions and The Planning Process of The Virginia CCC State Park Master Plans, 1933–1942*. University of Virginia, School of Architecture Independent Study, 1984.

Nutting, Wallace. *Virginia Beautiful*. New York: Old America Company, 1930.

Smith, Langdon. *The Democratization of Nature: State Park Development During The New Deal*. University of Kansas, Department of Geography, 2002.

Sturgill, Mack. *Hungry Mother: History and Legends*, Friends of Hungry Mother, Second Edition, 2001.

United States Department of the Interior. *National Register of Historic Places Inventory-Nomination Forms*: Bear Creek Lake, Douthat, Fairy Stone, Holliday Lake, Hungry Mother, Sailor's Creek Battlefield, Seashore, Staunton River, Twin Lakes, and Westmoreland State Parks, various dates.

Virginia State Park Staff. *Histories of Individual State Parks*, 2010.

ABOUT THE VIRGINIA ASSOCIATION FOR PARKS

Far and away the best prize that life has to offer is the chance to work hard at work worth doing.

—Theodore Roosevelt

Founded in 1997, VAFP is a volunteer, nonprofit, umbrella organization for the citizen support groups and individuals supporting state parks, natural areas, and national parks, monuments, and historic sites across the commonwealth. To learn more, go to: www.virginiaparks.org.

VAFP MEETING. Johnny Finch, a founding member and president, speaks at a recent meeting. VAFP holds annual spring and fall conferences to update members on challenges and opportunities for parks in Virginia. (Photograph courtesy DCR.)

Visit us at
arcadiapublishing.com

....

Printed in the USA
CPSIA information can be obtained
at www.ICGtesting.com
LVHW071026211223
766685LV00056B/928

9 781531 658359